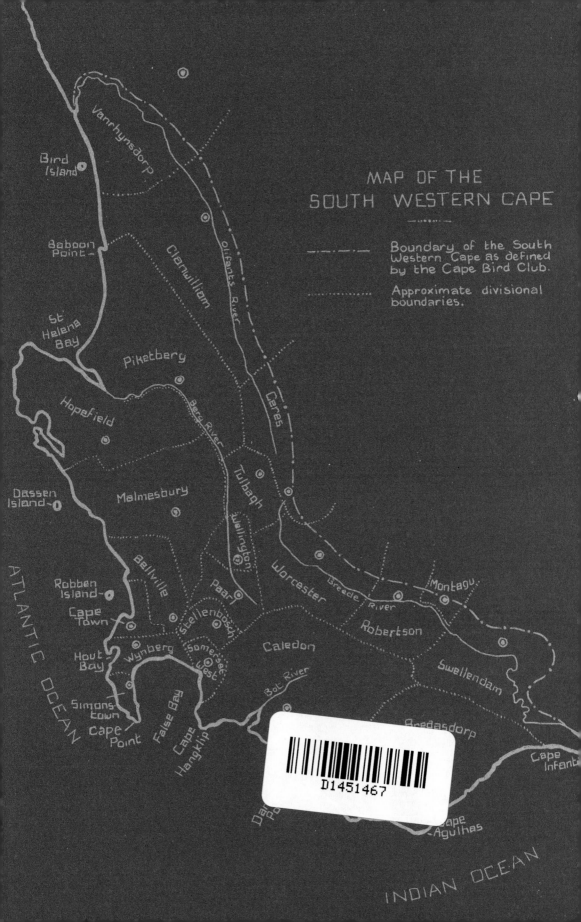

MAP OF THE
SOUTH WESTERN CAPE
— · — · —

— — — Boundary of the South
Western Cape as defined
by the Cape Bird Club.

············· Approximate divisional
boundaries.

Vanrhynsdorp

Bird
Island

Baboon
Point

St
Helena
Bay

Olifants River

Clanwilliam

Piketberg

Ceres

Hopefield

Berg River

Dassen
Island

Malmesbury

Tulbagh

Wellington

ATLANTIC OCEAN

Robben
Island

Bellville

Paarl

Worcester

Breede River

Montagu

Cape
Town

Stellenbosch

Robertson

Swellendam

Hout
Bay

Wynberg

Somerset
West

Caledon

Simons-
town

False Bay

Bot River

Bredasdorp

Cape
Point

Cape
Hangklip

Cape
Infanta

Danger Point

Cape
Agulhas

INDIAN OCEAN

D1451467

BIRDS OF THE
SOUTH WESTERN CAPE

To Him
whose creation it is

BIRDS OF THE SOUTH WESTERN CAPE

JOY FRANDSEN

Sable Publishers

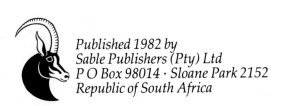

Published 1982 by
Sable Publishers (Pty) Ltd
P O Box 98014 · Sloane Park 2152
Republic of South Africa

© *Joy Frandsen*

Designed by Benni Hotz

Reproduction & typesetting by Hirt et Carter (Pty) Ltd · Cape Town

Printed and bound by Creda Press (Pty) Ltd · Cape Town

Deluxe Edition · Bound by Peter Carstens · Johannesburg

ISBN 0 620 06260 6

CONTENTS

ACKNOWLEDGEMENTS

I would like to thank my husband Robin for the encouragement
he gave me to start work on this book and for his untiring effort in
collecting the excellent photographs used throughout.

Thanks go also to my mother, to members of my family, and to
friends, who have, by their interest, promoted my own enthusiasm,
which has lent wings to the task.

It was Dr. Guy Currie of Cape Town who channelled the original idea
of a book encompassing a wider geographical boundary, into a more
definite area, and suggested that it be concentrated in the south
western Cape. This has made it possible to produce a detailed book
without making it too bulky for easy handling in the field.

Much thanks and appreciation go to Nico and Ella Myburgh
of Somerset West, for their interest and assistance, their warm
hospitality, and for the hours spent studying photographs.

I should like to express my thanks to Mr. Ken Newman,
and to the Trustees of the John Voelcker Bird Book Fund,
for the use of the plates to illustrate the Swifts — which were
not inclined to sit and pose for the camera!

In particular, while acknowledging the truly outstanding
contributions made by all the photographers represented in this
book, I want to say what a real joy it has been to work from such
magnificent material.

PHOTOGRAPHIC ACKNOWLEDGEMENTS

The following list of photographs have been selected from the great many submitted for inclusion in this book:

R. Abrams	:	6
J. Brooks	:	116 (a & b)
J. Cooper	:	13
P. Ginn	:	79, 181 (a), 232.
J. Harvey	:	115, 155 (b), 204 (a).
E. & D. Hosking	:	7 (a & b), 72, 102, 103, 105, 110, 111, 182, 216 (b).
A. Joubert	:	260
J. Kloppers	:	159
T. Longrigg	:	4, 41, 43, 92, 95, 106, 123, 124, 179, 180, 183, 185, 186, 194, 202, 210, 212, 231.
G. McIlleron	:	136, 138, 252, 256.
N. Myburgh	:	3, 5, 16, 17, 18, 20, 21 (a & b), 22, 23 (a & b), 24, 25, 26, 27, 28, 29, 30, 31, 33 (a & b), 34, 35, 36, 37, 40, 44, 45, 50 (b), 51, 55, 56 (b), 58, 59, 60, 63, 65, 66, 67, 68, 70 (a & b), 75, 76, 77, 78, 80, 81, 82, 83; 86 (a & b), 88, 90, 91, 93, 94, 96, 97, 98, 99, 100, 101, 104, 108, 109, 113, 119 (a), 121, 122, 125, 126, 127, 128 (a & b), 129, 130, 131, 132 (a & b), 133, 134, 135, 137 (a & b), 139, 140, 143 (a & b), 144 (a & b), 145, 151, 154, 155 (a), 156, 157, 158, 160, 161, 162, 164, 165 (a & b), 166, 167, 168, 170, 171, 172, 173, 175, 178, 187, 188, 189, 190, 191 (b), 192, 193, 195, 196, 198, 199, 200, 204 (b), 205, 206, 207, 208, 209, 211, 213, 214, 215, 216 (a), 217, 218, 219, 220, 221 (a & b), 222 (a & b), 223, 224, 227, 228, 229, 230, 233, 234, 237, 238 (a & b), 239 (a & b), 240 (a & b), 241, 242, 243, 244 (a & b), 245 (a & b), 246 (a & b), 248, 250 (a & b), 251, 253, 254 (a & b), 255 (a & b), 257, 259, 261, 262.
W. Nichol	:	74, 152.
D. Steele	:	191 (a), 258.
P. Steyn	:	2, 9, 10, 14, 15, 19, 32, 38, 39, 42, 48, 52, 53, 54, 56 (a), 62, 69, 71, 84, 85, 107, 141, 142, 153, 174, 177, 181 (b), 184, 201, 203.
W. Tarboton	:	64, 73, 197.
F. Weber	:	47, 50 (a), 57, 89, 112, 120, 163, 169, 176.
T. Williams	:	8, 11, 12, 118, 119 (b).
H. von Hörsten	:	1, 46, 49, 114, 225, 226, 236, 247, 249.
L. von Hörsten	:	61, 235.
Front cover	:	N. Myburgh
Title page	:	H. von Hörsten

Back cover (top left, clockwise): H. von Hörsten, N. Myburgh, H. von Hörsten, N. Myburgh

FOREWORD

Professor John Miall Winterbottom B.Sc. Ph.D (Univ. of London).
First Director of Percy Fitzpatrick Institute of African Ornithology, University of Cape Town.
Past President of the South African Ornithological Society.

It has been said, "of the making of books there is no end"; and recently we have begun to think that is true of bird books in particular. But there is always room for another if it is good enough – and this book certainly is. It covers 262 species, with about 300 photographs. The text is concise, non-technical and helpful; the pictures, by some of the best bird-photographers in South Africa, are not only beautiful but really valuable aids to identification. I have always been a bit suspicious of photographs as a means of identification – all too often, however decorative they may be, they do not show the diagnostic points that distinguish one species from another. This criticism does not apply to the photographs in this book, which have contrived to show the essentials without spoiling the picture. Look at the portrait of the Whimbrel, for instance, and notice how the photographer has managed to get in the pale streak on the top of the head, yet the bird is in a perfectly natural position.

The book is orientated in the South West Cape but, although it includes local specialities like the Orange-breasted Sunbird and the Rock Jumper, most of the species discussed have a much wider range – some of them all over South Africa. So, while the book is invaluable for bird-watchers in the Cape Town area, it will also be useful to lovers of birds all over the country. It fills a real gap in our literature, both Bolster's and my own books on the area, besides being on a more modest scale, having been out of print for many years.

I congratulate the author, photographers and publishers on a first-rate job.

J. M. Winterbottom

INTRODUCTION

One of the great heritages of the south western Cape is its abundant
bird life, comprising approximately two hundred and sixty two species,
some resident, some intercontinental migrants, all adding to the
kaleidoscope of natural beauty so abundantly evident in this spectacular
part of southern Africa.

The aim of this book is to present a detailed and comprehensive descriptive
work on this aspect of the natural history of the area, and to further
substantiate these descriptions with one or more colour photographs of
outstanding merit, highlighting important distinguishing features of each
species. The species are grouped in ornithological families and illustrated in
their natural setting of sea or sandy beach, on rocks, in reed-fringed pools,
on trees overhanging rivers, in thick grass, on a perch in dense bush, in
typical Fynbos, in the forests, mountainous terrain or dry arid areas, which
together make up this part of the Cape.

The birds are numbered and indexed for quick reference, both in English and
Afrikaans, with the recognised numbering of Robert's Birds of South Africa
included as well. Latin names have been brought up to date, descriptions
have been intentionally kept fairly short, clear and concise, so that with the
addition of further information as regards average length, young birds, flight
patterns, natural habitat, courtship, breeding, migration, the calls, and many
interesting patterns of behaviour, this volume will still remain compact
enough for easy handling in the field. The nest and the eggs have not been
forgotten and there are many interesting photographs of adults and chicks at
the nest, and of eggs laid in a hollow in a stretch of sand, in a protective ring
of stones, in the cleft of a rock, or carefully hidden in a rather more
conventional nest.

The rich bounty of bird life in the south western Cape, with many of the
birds inhabiting widespread areas throughout South Africa, has now been
comprehensively recorded in colour photography of the highest standard,
and it is hoped that this book will increase the enjoyment of existing
committed bird lovers, and will so delight those hesitating on the verge of
becoming interested, that they may become similarly captivated and find
profound pleasure in this fascinating subject.

Joy Frandsen

1. Jackass Penguin *Spheniscus demersus* 60 cm R2

Field Identification: The stocky Jackass Penguin has a black head with a distinct broad white stripe from over the eye down to the white neck and throat, and a conspicuous black inverted horseshoe stripe over the white chest which is sparsely spotted with black. The photograph shows an interesting aberration in which one of the penguins has a double stripe on the chest. The upper parts are black and the lower back and rump are washed with silvery grey. The bill is black with a grey band near the tip, the eyes hazel surrounded by pink skin, legs and webbed feet black, mottled with pink. Females are similar and young penguins have sides of face dusky and very little white above the eye. Nestlings are sooty brown above and off-white below.

Distribution: A flightless sea-bird found on the south and west coasts and on the coastal islands. Usually found within 12 km of the coast. Birds ringed in the south western Cape have been recovered from as far afield as East London and Swakopmund.

Notes: When seen waddling along on land with their very short legs they have a very upright stance. They swim under water using flippers and their webbed feet. Feed on small fish such as pilchards and small crayfish. Breed in large colonies on the guano islands mainly from January to May, making nests in burrows dug out of hard sand, or in a protected place between boulders lined with quills, pieces of seaweed, and other flotsam. Eggs are white and usually number two. The name is derived from the fact that they utter a loud bray like a donkey – a sound which is usually heard only at night. An aquatic bird swimming rapidly very low in the water, diving quickly and quietly. Sometimes called the English Jackass. In Afrikaans: Pikkewyn, in Xhosa: in-Guza.

2. Rockhopper Penguin *Eudyptes chrysocone* 56 cm R3

Field Identification: A little smaller than the Jackass Penguin and with very distinctive pale yellow plumes extending from the yellow stripe above the eyes, and with black plumes forming side crests. The head, neck and upper parts are black with upper chest and belly plain white. The bill is a dull tannish pink with the upper portion

deeply grooved. The eyes are a dull rose red colour, feet pink with black claw-like tips. Female is slightly smaller than the male. Young birds lack black on front neck.

Distribution: A very rare straggler to the south western Cape coast but there are records mainly of moulting juveniles in January and February from Table Bay to Hermanus.

Notes: On the rare occasions that this bird is seen it has proved to be quite indifferent to the presence of human beings. Inhabits islands of the southern oceans, ranging north to 30° south in winter. Rockhopper penguins feed on small fish, crustacea and various molluscs. Predators on this species are giant petrels, sea lions, fur seals and possibly sharks and killer whales. In Afrikaans: Geel-kuif-pikkewyn.

3. Great Crested Grebe *Podiceps cristatus* 50 cm R4

Field Identification: Duck-sized but immediately distinguished from ducks by the long thin neck and large head. When breeding the adult has conspicuous chestnut frills broadly edged with black on either side of the head, and a black tuft on either side of the crown. Sides of head and throat are offwhite, flanks tinged with chestnut, back and rump dark greyish brown, underparts silky white. Eyes deep red, legs black, bill dark brownish grey with a slight reddish tinge. A distinctive white bar is seen at the base of the wings when in flight and the silhouette shows the legs projecting beyond the tail feathers. The photograph shows a young bird going for a ride on the back of the adult. The bare pink patch on the crown is clearly visible as well as the distinct black and white colouring on the head. Adult birds of both sexes are similar.

Distribution: Prefers large sheets of open fresh water such as large vleis and dams. Its numbers fluctuate tremendously from year to year on any one particular vlei.

Notes: The Great Crested Grebe is to be seen in full breeding plumage during the period from September to November. There is an elaborate courtship display during which the birds swim towards each other, their bills skimming the water and their heads moving jerkily. They usually nest on semi-floating islands built of reeds and water plants and parent birds invariably cover eggs before leaving the nest. They feed on small fish and insects as well as larvae and crustacea. Found on large vleis swimming far from the water's edge either singly, in pairs, or in family groups. During the breeding period they utter a low-pitched 'keek keek'. In Afrikaans: Kuifkop-duikertjie.

4. Blacknecked Grebe *Podiceps nigricollis* 28 cm R5

Field Identification: Distinguished from the Dabchick in the field by its larger size and by its white flanks and belly. In breeding plumage its head is slightly crested with a shining patch of golden chestnut feathers on the side. Non-breeding the throat, chest and sides of neck are white and there is no chestnut on sides of head or on flanks. The upper parts are greyish black, eyes bright crimson, bill and legs black.

Young birds are streaked on head, neck and body, and are brown above. The shape of the mandible gives the impression of a slightly upturned bill.

Distribution: Distributed on vleis in the south western Cape mainly in the summer months; also in flocks on the sea at Lambert's Bay in Spring. Prefers large reed-fringed lakes.

Notes: Has a characteristic habit of preening and floating on its side, exposing its silvery white flanks. The breeding time is irregular but is usually given as September to February and nesting takes place in colonies with from six to twenty five nests in one area. Eggs number two or three, yellowish brown and round at both ends. Feeds on small water animals and its voice is a quiet 'poo-eep' and a rapid clatter. In Afrikaans: Swartnek-duikertjie

5. Little Grebe *Tachybaptus ruficollis* 20 cm R6

Field Identification: Commonly known as the Dabchick and distinguished from the Blacknecked Grebe by being smaller in size, having a white spot at the base of the bill and smoky grey neck and sides. The chin, face, top of head and hind neck are black, the general colour being a blackish brown above and the belly silvery white, or white

tinged with brown. During the breeding season, as seen in the illustration, the plumage turns to a deep chestnut on the sides of the neck and the white spot at the gape is particularly noticeable. The sexes are alike. White secondaries are conspicuous in flight. Eyes brown, bill black tipped with white, legs black. Young birds have similar colouring to the non-breeding adults but with streaks of black on neck and head.

Distribution: Throughout the area and common on permanent vleis and swamps.

Notes: Often seen in pairs or small family parties and has a characteristic of 'standing' on the water, flapping its wings vigorously or running along the water surface and coming to a skidding halt. Feeds mainly on small frogs and water insects and when feeding undisturbed will dive down into the water with scarcely a ripple. Its call can be described as a descending trill like a musical laugh, but an alarm note is a loud sharp 'chick'. Breeds August to February and constructs a floating nest of wet weeds built about three centimetres above the water around the edges, with the hollow at water level. The newly laid eggs, numbering three to six, are powder blue but turn ivory in a few days. In Afrikaans: Klein Duikertjie, in Xhosa: u-Nolwibili, in Sotho: le-Fuli.

6. Wandering Albatross *Diomedea exulans* 130 cm R7

Field Identification: The largest flying bird alive today with a wingspan up to 3,25 metres. An adult male is all white except for black tips to the wings. The female may have a dark cap and black markings on upper wings and back, with white under the wings. Young birds are brown with conspicuously contrasting white faces. The bill is pale pink, the legs a pale flesh colour tinged with blue, the eyes brown.

Distribution: A pelagic species recorded throughout the year but most usually from October to December. The Wandering Albatross seldom comes inshore, remaining beyond five kilometres from land, unless driven in occasionally in stormy weather.

Notes: These fascinating birds may live for more than thirty five years, breeding in colonies on subantarctic islands. They have an elaborate courtship ritual with up to six pairs taking part in bowing, dancing and bill-clapping and sometimes pairs remain together for their entire lifespan. One egg is laid in November, which is greatly endangered by being trampled or dislodged and eaten by skuas. If the egg is hatched the parents feed the chick until the following September and it takes ten years before the young bird has adult plumage. The pair return to the original nest site after migrating and undergoing a moult. The voice sounds like a loud bray or a coughing grunt. They feed mostly at night on surface fish and squid. Other names are the Snowy or White-winged Albatross and the Cape sheep. In Afrikaans: Groot Albatros.

7. Blackbrowed Albatross *Diomedea melanophris* 85–95 cm R8

Field Identification: The entire head, neck and underparts white. Viewed from above in flight the slaty black wing colour extends across the back in a continuous band, with lower rump white and tail feathers slate grey. From beneath, as shown in

the photograph there is a broader edging of black on the forward edge of the wings than that on the back edge and the centre portion is white; the legs extend to the black edge of the tail. There is a distinctive black line through the eye, which is brown, and the thick pink-tipped yellow bill is curved at the end, legs pinky white to yellow. The sexes are similar and immature birds are greyish on the neck and head, the underwing is darker and the beak is olivy grey with a darker tip. The photographs were taken on the Falkland Islands.

Distribution: Found off the coast as far as Walvis Bay, chiefly during the summer months. More numerous than the Wandering Albatross. A common pelagic species coming close inshore when following ships into bays and found in considerable numbers on the trawling grounds off Cape Town. Birds ringed on the South Georgia Islands have been recovered in Table Bay.

Notes: Feed on fish offal from trawlers, surface fish and squid. Breed in colonies on subantarctic islands. Have a guttural grunting or cackling voice when squabbling over food and a braying note when displaying in the breeding season. Lays one white egg which is tinged with pink and has reddish brown markings at the larger end. The nest is a raised mound of mud lined with feathers or vegetable matter. In Afrikaans: Malmok.

8. Greyheaded Albatross *Diomedea chrysostoma* 82 cm R9

Field Identification: Easily identified by its very pale grey head with a dark patch in front of and over the eye area. Wings blackish brown above, back and tail feathers dark grey and underparts white. The bill is black and has unusual yellow ridges along the upper and lower central edges forming a central stripe, and has a slightly red tip. Eyes are brown with a dark line over the top. Legs and webbed feet are pale fleshy blue. Females are similar but smaller, and immature birds are leaden grey with upper wings brown and black bills.

Distribution: Occurs on the Antarctic oceans as far north as the Cape. A rare species recorded from the western Cape and Algoa Bay. Recorded off the continental shelf and further out to sea.

Notes: Seen more often singly than in groups. Feeds on fish, squid, dead seabirds and even galley scraps. Breed on subantarctic islands. Males have a courtship display stretching their bills towards one another, holding them motionless, then braying, bowing, fanning their tails, preening and parading around the females. One brown-banded white egg is laid in a mud nest lined with vegetable matter. The call is a braying, guttural sound. In Afrikaans: Gryskop-malmok.

9. Yellownosed Albatross *Diomedea chlororhynchos* 75 cm R10

Field Identification: Both male and female have white head and neck with very pale grey nape, wings blackish-brown above, back and tail dark grey. The bill is noticeably slender, lacking the yellow on the bottom edge of mandible, as seen in the

Greyheaded Albatross, but having a yellow stripe down the centre of the upper mandible and an orange tip. Underparts and underwings white, the latter having a black margin all round, thicker on the forward edge. Eyes brown, legs and webbed feet pale flesh with a bluish tinge. Young birds resemble adults but have plain black bills.

Distribution: Found all year round but more usually in summer some distance offshore, especially in the trawling areas. Less common than the Blackbrowed Albatross.

Notes: A fairly common pelagic species feeding on offal, squid and large shrimps. Like most albatross species they commonly follow ships and sometimes their attention around fishing boats can become a nuisance. They have a hoarse guttural call when fighting over food or when courting, also a bleating cry. In Afrikaans: Geelbekmalmok.

10. Sooty Albatross *Phoebetria fusca* 85 cm R12

Field Identification: Sooty grey in colour, slightly lighter on back and belly. There is a long wedge-shaped tail and an incomplete white ring around the eye. This description fits both the Sooty Albatross and the Lightmantled Sooty Albatross, distinguishing them from other albatross species. The latter species however has an almost offwhite back and chest and no yellow on the bill. The Sooty Albatross, illustrated here, has a black bill with a yellow or orange line along the lower mandible and slightly pinkish grey legs. Eyes are brown. The wide yet narrow-winged wingspan is a distinguishing feature in flight. Chicks are grey with white faces.

Distribution: A pelagic migrant found south of Cape Agulhas in the winter months also recorded between Robben Island and Dassen Island in May. Obviously difficult to sight or photograph but this species does sometimes follow ships in the area.

Notes: The two species described here have a beautiful gliding flight with slow wheeling turns, using their large webbed feet as brakes. Breed on the subantarctic islands of Marion Island and Gough Island, usually making their nest in ridges or gullies overlooking a steep drop to the sea. Nests are usually hidden by thick vegetation. When threatened they vomit the foul-smelling remnants of their meals as a means of defence. In Afrikaans: Bruin Malmok.

11. Southern Giant Petrel *Macronectes giganteus* 89 cm R13

Field Identification: There are two phases of this species one being wholly white and sparingly flecked on the body with dark grey, but the other darker phase illustrated here is the more common, the lower back and flight feathers being either sooty black or a mixed grey and brown with lighter foreparts, some individuals being very light and almost white on head and breast but speckled with black and brown as shown. Eyes are dark brown, bill with large tubular nostrils in pinkish horn sometimes tipped with pale green, tail wedge-shaped. In this species males are considerably larger than females and young birds of the white plumaged variety are white, whereas the young of the dark plumaged variety are a glossy blackish brown becoming lighter as they grow older.

Distribution: Recorded throughout the year along the Cape coast but rarely from December to April during which time they breed on southern islands. Usually sighted singly, fairly close inshore and near harbours. Nearly all birds sighted are immature.

Notes: In flight the head is bent downwards giving a hunchbacked, stiff appearance. Marauders feeding on offal, carrion, small sea-birds – even smaller petrels or penquin chicks. Characteristically they first alight fairly close to food and swim towards it. A guttural raucous 'hu hu hu' is made by this species commonly known to fishermen as 'The Stinker' due to its obnoxious habit of vomiting vile-smelling substances in the direction of a suspected enemy. In Afrikaans: Nellie.

12. Softplumaged Petrel *Pterodroma mollis* 35 cm R19

Field Identification: Light grey head with protruding, lightly speckled forehead and a broad sooty stripe through the eye. Mantle and upper parts grey with wings greyish black and underparts white except for a narrow slate-grey chest band. Dark wing

coverts form an M on back of open wings in flight. Eyes brown, bill black, legs flesh with black claws.

Distribution: A pelagic visitor to offshore waters as far as 170 kms and further, usually from May to October. Found inshore occasionally probably as the result of heavy stormy weather.

Notes: An offshore pelagic species that has been recorded at various times throughout the year but which is nevertheless uncommon. Does not follow boats but when sighted it is seen to have a graceful rapid flight following a typical zigzag route. In Afrikaans: Donsveer-stormvoël.

13. Whitechinned Petrel *Procellaria aequinoctialis* 57 cm R23

Field Identification: The commonest Petrel off the south western Cape coast, rather plain with feathers of sooty black tinged with chocolate brown. The name is derived

from a distinctive white chin patch which varies in extent from bird to bird. The thick hooked beak is a pale greenish or yellowish horn, eyes brown and legs and webbed feet black. Females and young birds are similar.
Distribution: Commonly found off the coast but fairly near to land.
Notes: Cheeky, fearless birds scavenging on offal thrown from ships and coming into harbours for that purpose. Dive well and will swim strongly to catch young fish. Also feed on small crabs and squid. In Afrikaans: Bassiaan.

14. Great Shearwater *Puffinus gravis* 45 cm R25

Field Identification: Upper parts dark brownish grey but juvenile birds have upper parts grey with pale feather edging as seen in the photograph. White underwing-coverts and white on upper tail-coverts. Adult birds are darkest on head and the white collar effect around the neck makes the dark-capped appearance very conspicuous. Underparts white with dark flecks, legs flesh coloured with outer edge brownish-black. Bill dark greyish horn.
Distribution: During the period from October to January it is sometimes very abundant off the Peninsula, Dassen Island and Cape Columbine and has even been seen in Table Bay docks. Stragglers are sometimes seen from February to September. A pelagic species common offshore.

Notes: During the winter large rafts of this species are a feature on the trawling grounds. The flight pattern is low and skimming with quick wing-beats, a flap and then a smooth glide. Fly straight into the water for food. Breeding takes place on islands in the southern seas but during the southern winter they will migrate as far north as Greenland. In Afrikaans: Groot Pylstormvoël.

15. White Pelican *Pelecanus onocrotalus* 180 cm R42

Field Identification: A large white aquatic bird with short pinkish straw legs and webbed feet, a long purplish white bill with yellow edges and a naked yellow pouch suspended from the lower mandible. Primaries and wing coverts black. In flight the undersides of the wings show clearly the forward section white and the back portion

black. The crest of the female is slightly larger and young birds are brownish above.

Distribution: Found is shallow coastal and inland waters. Chiefly a freshwater species of the larger vleis, formerly breeding on Seal Island in False Bay and now found breeding on Dassen Island in summer.

Notes: During the breeding season the white colouring is tinged with pink and in both sexes there is a longer crest. The nest is either a shallow scraped hole or a dirty ring of seaweed with added feathers. Eggs are found in January, two or three of a chalky white colour, discoloured by guano. Large numbers of White Pelicans drive shoals of fish into shallow waters where they scoop them up into their pouches. They also eat young birds. Do not make much sound except to grunt at nesting sites. In Afrikaans: Wit Pelikaan, and in Xhosa: Ingcwangube.

16. Cape Gannet *Morus capensis* 90 cms R44

Field Identification: The Cape Gannet is a white marine bird with long wings edged with black and the tail feathers, legs and webbed feet also black. The bare skin sur-

rounding the eye and down the centre of the neck is black, with the eye itself ringed with light blue. There is a pale yellow shading on the crown and the back of the neck and the general plumage of the bird has a distinctive gleaming quality. The female is similar and young birds are brownish speckled with white.

Distribution: Found in coastal waters throughout the year as far as 160 kms offshore.

Notes: Breed on Bird Island and Malgas Island from September to March. Thousands gather making their nests from guano and debris which is formed into a hollowed mound. Interestingly the single egg laid is incubated by the birds' feet. It is initially bluish-white but later becomes dirty and covered in guano. The voice is a loud raucous 'kara-kara-kara-kara'. Large numbers of these birds are seen following shoals of fish as their diet consists of surface fish like pilchard, mullet, mackerel and maasbanker as well as cephalopods. Characteristically they will be seen gliding up into the air in an arc and diving onto their prey from a considerable height. In Afrikaans: Malgas, in Xhosa: Umkholonjane.

17. Whitebreasted Cormorant *Phalacrocorax carbo* 90 cm R47

Field Identification: The Whitebreasted Cormorant is the largest of the Cormorants and is easily identified as it has a relatively short tail and white on the breast in sharp contrast to the glossy greenish black of the rest of its plumage. During the breeding season there is also a white patch on each thigh and the entire throat is similarly white. Non-breeding birds are brownish on sides of head and neck. The sharply hooked beak is grey, eyes greenish, naked lores yellow, pouch greenish grey, legs and webbed feet black. The sexes are alike and nestlings are sooty brown becoming offwhite below before reaching maturity.

Distribution: To be found on salt and fresh water, off the Cape coast within a distance of 3 kms, on offshore islands, on seashore rocks and on permanent rather than temporary inland vleis. They appear to live in permanently separated colonies, some in seawater and others in fresh water habitats.

Notes: Unlike other species of aquatic birds Cormorant's feathers get wet when in contact with water for long, and they are often seen with their wings partly extended perched on a rock while they dry off. Breed throughout the year but August or January are peak periods. Nests are built in colonies on coastal islands or occasionally on coastal cliffs. They are formed from sticks which become covered in guano, but old nests are often used again, relined with bits of seaweed or other vegetable matter. Four eggs are laid, of a chalky white colour. This species swims low in the water, with the body submerged, and feeds on small fish. The call is merely a low grunt at the nesting site. In Afrikaans: Witbors-duiker, in Xhosa: Ugwidi.

18. Cape Cormorant *Phalacrocorax capensis* 64 cm R48

Field Identification: Distinguished by plain dark colouring, naked yellow lores and a short-tailed appearance. Young or non-breeding birds are brown in colour, lighter brown on throat and chest. During the breeding period from September to February they are a uniform black, as seen in the photograph, the sexes alike. Eyes greenish, hooked beak black, naked lores and pouch orangy yellow, legs and webbed feet black.

Distribution: Abundant and resident along the entire south western Cape coast and up to 50 kms out to sea. Especially large flocks are to be seen along the northern shore of False Bay and on the Strandfontein Sewage Works, while individual birds are found to rest for a few days at a time at the Rondevlei Bird Sanctuary.

Notes: A marine species being colonial breeders on islands in Saldanha Bay and on the cliffs of the Cape of Good Hope Nature Reserve, where they breed in immense numbers, particularly from September to November, making their nests from seaweed and sticks. Eggs number two or three and are chalky white. During the summer months in the Cape 'trekking' is often seen, with hundreds or even thousands of birds crossing the water, following in long lines, dipping and rising. When they discover a shoal of fish they settle, dive and surface with great activity. Have also been known to eat mussels and crabs. They make no sound. In Afrikaans: Trekduiker, in Xhosa: Ugwidi.

19. Bank Cormorant *Phalacrocorax neglectus* 75 cm R49

Field Identification: Distinguishable from other Cormorants because it is totally a gleaming black and lacks the naked yellow lores. Rather large with a heavy body. Occasionally individuals have a white marking on the rump. The hooked bill, feet and legs are also black. Eyes red, pouch black. Albinistic birds have been seen occasionally.

Distribution: A resident marine species domiciled on offshore islands and found all along the south western Cape coast from Swakopmund to as far south as Agulhas but more often no further south than the Cape Peninsula. Have been recorded up to 120 kms out to sea but this is very unusual, the usual range being up to 9 kms from shore.

Notes: This black aquatic bird flies with neck stretched forward and a rapid wingbeat. Breeding time appears to be any month in the year except April, August or November. Nests are made from red algae collected from offshore areas and are to be seen on the same big boulders year after year. Often when they leave their nests unguarded their neighbours steal the material for their own nests. Eggs number two or three and are chalky white. In Afrikaans: Bankduiker.

20. Reed Cormorant *Phalacrocorax africanus* 60 cm R50

Field Identification: A long tailed cormorant with a short neck and rather shorter yet typical cormorant bill, hooked at the tip. When in full breeding plumage the Reed Cormorant is a glossy black, with bronze grey markings on the back and wings, clearly illustrated in the photograph. The crest when breeding is longer, in fact it is practically absent for the remaining part of the year. Eyes are red, naked lores yellowy red, bill dark blackish above and lighter horn below, with a black tip, legs and webbed feet black. The sexes are similar and young birds have breast offwhite, throat and belly light brown. The marine birds form a separate species, *coronatus* (R61) the Crowned Cormorants, which breed along the west coast and on an off-shore island near Cape Hangklip.

Distribution: The typical Reed Cormorant is found on all fresh waters in the area and breeds in colonies, often mixed with herons and egrets, from September to December. It is also regular on tidal mud-flats and lagoons. A bird ringed at Rondevlei was re-covered near Swellendam. Flies high in the sky when travelling from one fishing water to an-other.

Notes: Exceptionally good swim-mers and divers, living on fish, frogs, and other prey pursued under water. On land they wad-dle about with a duck-like gait, and are seen characteristically drying their feathers with wings outstretched, as seen here, while perched on rocks or trees. Nests are constructed from platforms of sticks and are usually found on rocky ledges, containing two to four elongated bluish white eggs. In Afrikaans: Rietduiker.

21. Darter *Anhinga melanogaster rufa* 83 cm R52

Field Identification: It would be difficult to confuse the Darter with any other species due to its long thin bill, small head and long thin curved neck. The sharp point of the bill separates it from the Cormorants. The male and female differ when breeding, the male having a black crown and hind neck separated half the way down from the chestnut throat by a white stripe, as can be seen in the photograph. The female has crown and back of neck brown with lower neck fawn. Young birds have neck and throat offwhite with body fawn and darker flanks.

Distribution: Seen regularly on larger sheets of water throughout the south western Cape.

Notes: Found resting on a rock or tree close to a quiet stretch of water, either alone or in groups. The Darter is a strong swimmer and will slide into the water soundlessly, swimming with the entire body submerged and nothing but the small head and long

sharp bill to be seen. Colonial nesters often found nesting near Cormorants. The nests are large, made from reeds and twigs, containing from three to five smooth white elongated eggs. Darter feed on fish and frogs caught with their long pointed bills while swimming underwater. Their cry is a raucous quack. In Afrikaans: Slanghalsvoël, in Xhosa: Ivusi.

22. Grey Heron *Ardea Cinerea* 100 cm R54

Field Identification: In accordance with its name the general impression is grey on the upper parts of the body but with white head and chest accented with a heavy black streak extending from over the eye to the back of the head and ending with a black plume. There is also a band of black streaks extending down the neck and breast. Immature birds have the head and neck more grey and may lack the plume; the bill and legs are a greenish grey. Mature birds have bill yellowish, legs greenish yellow, eyes yellow. When in flight the wings seen from beneath are grey.

Distribution: Found in both fresh and salt water environments, on lagoons, mud-flats, permanent and temporary vleis, and on ploughed fields during the winter months.

Notes: Often seen standing motionless in shallow water alert for any movement which would indicate the presence of frogs, crabs, fish or insects. On land will also eat small rats, moles or birds. A typical posture is with the head drawn back into the shoulders, in which position it is also seen in flight, with legs extended. A solitary bird, seemingly shy and not very plentiful. Breeds from July to February commonly in colonial nests. When returning to the nest there is usually much commotion with vociferous calls and displaying of the crests and plumes. The nests are large, constructed from sticks and found in trees or reed beds. Eggs number from two to four and are a pale blue. In Afrikaans: Blou Reier, in Sotho: Kokolofitoe, in Xhosa: Ukhwalimanzi.

23. Blackheaded Heron *Ardea melanocephala* 96 cm R55

Field Identification: A large mainly grey bird with a black plume falling over the black crown and long black neck. The throat is white and the dark grey front of the lower neck is streaked with white. The bill is grey, as distinct from the yellow bill of the Grey Heron. When in flight the white underwing-coverts and black flight feathers are clearly evident. The sexes are alike. This species usually has yellow eyes but the illustration shows an interesting variation in which the bird has red eyes. Long legs and feet black. Young birds are grey instead of black on head and neck.

Distribution: Seen more often away from water in pasture land and orchards than the Grey Heron and seen regularly in the south western Cape. A bird ringed. at Rondevlei was recovered at Barrydale.

Notes: The Blackheaded Heron has a fast wingbeat and a typical heron flight. Quite cunning and quiet when hunting for food and very useful to man since it feeds on rodents as well as insects and lizards. Breeds from June to January, with a peak in October, in mixed heronries. Builds nests in trees or reed beds and eggs number two to four, of a pale blue colour. Inclined to make various croaking sounds in the nesting area and nestlings keep up a persistent 'cack-cack-cack'. In Afrikaans: Swartkopreier, in Xhosa: Ukhwalimanzi, in Sotho: Kokolofitoe.

♀

20

24. Purple Heron *Ardea purpurea* 89 cm R57

Field Identification: Easily identified by the long thin almost snake-like silhouette of bill, head and neck. Forehead and crown black with slight black crest on the back of the head. The very long curved neck is chestnut behind striped with black, chin and front of neck white with sparse lines of downward streaks. The hunched back, wings and tail are purplish grey. Non-breeding birds are brown with a purplish grey neck. This species has noticeably large black feet and when in flight there is a distinct downward bulge of the neck. Eyes yellow, bill greyish brown above and yellow below, legs yellow at the top with the front lower part blackish brown, the back part yellow.

Distribution: Widely distributed and seen on vleis and rivers where there are reed beds.

Notes: This species is a little difficult to spot due to its shy nature and the fact that it usually blends in so well with the colour of its surroundings, evident in the accompanying photograph. Breeds from September to October remaining solitary and building its nest, a large platform of twigs lined with reeds, in areas of dense reed beds. The eggs number two to five and are greenish blue. Feeds on fish, frogs and insects but has been known to take lizards, snakes or young chickens or ducklings. Its call is a hoarse 'kwaak'. In Afrikaans: Rooi Reier.

25. Great White Egret *Egretta alba* 95 cm R58

Field Identification: Distinguished from other Egrets by the fact that it is the largest of all the white members of the Heron family, but not quite as big as the Grey Heron. Unlike the Yellowbilled Egret, which is pinkish yellow on the legs above the tarsal joint, the Great White Egret has very long entirely black legs. The neck is long and slender, though often seen curved up against the body; the bill is yellow, except during the breeding season when it is black or black and yellow. The female is similar and young birds are covered in white down.

Distribution: Favours areas around flooded pans, vleis and rivers and considered a rare vagrant in the south western Cape, often confused with the Yellowbilled Egret.

Found throughout the area.

Notes: Most often seen alone but will roost and nest in community with other herons in large trees. Feeds on frogs, fish, other aquatic animals and insects, and when feeding has a peculiar stance, leaning slightly forward with neck well stretched out. Does not often make a sound but when heard it is a deep harsh 'aahrr'. Eggs have a coarse texture, number two to four, and are of a pale blue colour. In Afrikaans: Groot Witreier.

26. Little Egret *Egretta garzetta* 64 cm R59

Field Identification: A very beautiful bird in breeding plumage when it develops long graceful white plumes on the chest, crown and back. Normally when non-breeding an attractive slender bird, all white, with black bill and legs, and yellow feet. Smaller in size than the Great White Egret. Sexes are alike. Young birds have the lower mandible lighter.

Distribution: Seen regularly in the area on rocky coasts, tidal mud flats and in most fresh water situations. A young bird ringed at Rondevlei was found later in Mozambique.

Notes: Hunts for food in a more alert manner than other heron species, darting about with much agility and feeding on a variety of insects, shrimps, frogs, lizards and small fish. It has an almost comical high-stepping gait as it wades through water, its yellow feet becoming very conspicuous. Breeds from August to February. Nests are a shallow cup in a platform of sticks, with eggs numbering from two to four, palest greenish blue, almost white, incubated by both parents. In Afrikaans: Klein Witreier.

27. Yellowbilled Egret *Egretta intermedia* 68 cm R60

Field Identification: A medium sized Egret with a yellow bill and typical bend in the long neck. Develops beautiful long white plumes on back when breeding. Legs and feet are black, with a pinkish yellow portion above the tarsal joint. Eyes pale yellow with surrounding bare skin light grey. Long pointed bill yellow. Nestlings have biscuit coloured eyes and greenish grey legs.

Distribution: Found throughout the Cape at permanent vleis, irrigation lakes and farm dams. Never found away from water. A bird ringed at Rondevlei was recovered as far away as Zambia.

Notes: Breeds in mixed heronries from August to November in the Cape. The nest is a platform of sticks with a shallow cup containing two to four palest, almost white, greenish blue eggs. Feed on fish and tiny animals. Make no noise except during the breeding season when they utter a hoarse 'kwaak'. At this time they live in communities on trees and rocks and in the reed beds surrounding stretches of water. In Afrikaans: Geelbek-witreier.

28. Cattle Egret *Bubulcus Ibis* 54 cm R61

Field Identification: The Cattle Egret is the smallest of the Egrets, short-necked, stocky and with a shorter, thicker yellow bill, compared to the other species. Legs are yellow but are often discoloured with mud and dirt. Eyes pale yellow. Sexes alike. In breeding plumage there is an attractive pinkish orange plumage on crown, back and chest, in contrast to the general white. Non-breeding and young birds are plain white. Two varieties which do not fraternise are illustrated, the one with the yellow bill being the more common, both shown in breeding plumage.

Distribution: Found throughout the south western Cape at permanent vleis, large farm dams and in pasture lands with animals. It has increased in numbers vastly since the first recorded breeding in 1934, but has lessened again in areas where there is now less cattle farming.

Notes: Commonly known as the 'Tickbird' they are usually found in association with animals, particularly cattle, which they follow in order to collect the insects disturbed by the animal. They also settle on the backs of cattle to pick off ticks and flies. During the day they disperse in search of food but towards evening assemble in vast numbers at communal roosts in reed-beds and trees, usually alongside a stretch of water – although the Cattle Egret is the least aquatic of the Herons. Breeding season in the Cape is from June to December, the nest being a platform of sticks. Eggs are three to four, of a pale chalky blue. A harsh 'kraak' is the sound of alarm. It also makes other croaking sounds. In Afrikaans: Bosluisvoël, in Zulu: i-Landi.

29. Little Bittern *Ixobrychus minutus* 36 cm R67

Field Identification: A summer visitor to the Cape and rather difficult to spot due to the fact that they are mainly nocturnal. Another camouflaging trick is that they actually hide in reeds with their bills pointed upward parallel to the reed itself. Dark blackish green above with chestnut neck, light wing coverts and hind neck. Eyes orange; slender, long pointed bill dark above and reddish horn below, legs greyish yellow. In flight, and viewed from above, there is a dark crown, back, rump and tail with light head, neck and forepart of the wings. There is a very pale band of greyish blue across each wing and a terminal dark band, the legs extending behind the body. The female is light chestnut brown, the plumage edged with light beige, giving a mottled appearance and young birds are heavily streaked.
Distribution: Has been recorded widely in the south western Cape during the summer months and has bred at Lakeside, Faure, Rondevlei and near Stellenbosch.
Notes: Little Bitterns feed on spiders, grasshoppers, caterpillars, small fish, shrimps, frogs and lizards. They are difficult to flush from their hideaways in reed beds along streams and rivers. The alarm cry is a sharp 'squark' but at other times the sound is a 'crick' similar to the sound made by a frog. Nests are formed from twigs or roots

among reeds near to water and are placed near to the ground. Eggs number two or three and are white. In Afrikaans: Woudapie, In Xhosa: Ihashe.

30. Blackcrowned Night Heron
Nycticorax nycticorax **56 cm R69** *(Illustration overleaf)*
Field Identification: A rather beautiful bird in breeding plumage with crown and mantle black and a long white streamer on the nape. Sides of face, neck, chest and underparts are whitish and flight feathers grey. The bill is fairly heavy looking, all dark grey during the breeding season, but at other times black above and pinky beige below. Eyes are red, legs and feet yellow. The female is similar and young birds are greyish brown above with beige and white markings, while underparts are marked wih streaks of white and brown.
Distribution: Found usually at permanent vleis and seen most often on the branches of trees overhanging water. A bird ringed at Rondevlei was recorded in Mozambique a few months later.
Notes: Distinguishable when in flight, usually at dusk, by the large rounded shape of the wings. Is not inclined to stalk in the reeds for its food but will perch quietly waiting for fish or frogs to come into its orbit. Breeds in mixed heronries building

nests in trees or reed beds. The rather large nest of reeds and sticks will usually have from two to four eggs of palest green. At sunset it utters a hoarse 'quark', but when alarmed the sound is a sharp 'kwok-kwok'. In Afrikaans: Nagreier.

31. Hamerkop *Scopus umbretta* 56 cm R72

Field Identification: Brown all over with darker tail feathers and a large permanent crest on the head giving the shape from which its name is derived. Similar in size to the Cattle Egret. The bill is blackish and laterally compressed, the legs fairly thin and black. Female birds are similar but somewhat smaller, chicks have head, neck, back and wings white, but develop brown plumage and crest before they leave the nest.

Distribution: Found wherever there is water throughout the south western Cape. Used to breed commonly in the Stellenbosch area but there are no recent recorded breedings. The probable reason is nest predation by Egyptian Geese, Owls and the feral squirrel.

Notes: A very familiar bird near open shallow water, usually solitary or in pairs. In flight the wings appear broad and the neck is not pulled back but is only slightly curved. Hamerkops breed close to water in reed beds and low willow trees from July to January. They have a somewhat elaborate courting display which is accompanied by a monotonous croak. The nest is made from a variety of materials varying from sticks, grass, bits of rubbish, leather, old bones and even bits of cloth. It is constructed with a very inaccessible entrance, for protection from marauders and can take up to six months to construct. Eggs number three to six, white, but usually mud stained. The Hamerkop is regarded with superstitious awe by many Africans and they will even go so far as to remove their huts if a Hamerkop is seen to fly directly overhead. These birds will shuffle and stamp their feet in shallow water to disturb the insects, worms, fishes, tadpoles and frogs on which they feed. When excited or alarmed they utter a characteristic squeaky, whistling cry. In Afrikaans: Hamerkop, in Zulu: i-Tekwane, in Xhosa: Uthekwane.

32. Black Stork *Ciconia nigra* 122 cm R79

Field Identification: Head, neck, mantle, back, throat and upper chest as well as wings and tail a glossy brownish black with an iridescent sheen. Lower chest, belly and underparts white. Long legs coral, eyes brown ringed with naked red skin, long pointed bill and pouch coral. The female is similar and young birds have orange-tipped yellow beaks and are sooty brown with necks streaked.

Distribution: A summer visitor to vleis and lagoons but seen very occasionally in winter. Uncommon and usually non-breeding in the area although small resident populations have been discovered, breeding on cliffs.

Notes: Favours aquatic habitats and may be found at marshes, dams, rivers and estuaries usually singly or in small number, but

flocks of up to fifteen birds have been recorded. Live on fish and frogs as well as crabs and grasshoppers. A shy species with a quiet, guttural croak. In Afrikaans: Swart Ooievaar, in Xhosa: u-Nocufu.

33. White Stork *Ciconia ciconia* 117 cm R80

Field Identification: Clearly identified from the Yellowbilled Stork by the dark red bill. A large white stork with black flight feathers and tail, and long rose red legs which are frequently marked with powdery white from the bird's excrement. There is a connection between this phenomenon and the regulation of the bird's temperature. Very young chicks are speckled beige as seen in the line up of five in the photograph, but the other illustration shows young birds at the nest resembling the adult closely, except that the bills are black and the black plumage is slightly browner. Eyes dark brown, skin of pouch black anteriorly, red posteriorly.

Distribution: A Palaearctic migrant. Gathers at the end of a southern summer in great flocks to migrate northwards. Arrives at the Cape in mid-November and leaves about the end of March. A few have bred in the Bredasdorp district where the adult at the nest was actually photographed. A juvenile ringed in that area was recovered on the Zambia-Tanzania border. Usually found on open veld and grassland.

Notes: Appear sporadically where there are locust or caterpillar pests in abundance, in open veld and hence invaluable to man. Known to live over nineteen years. Food is derived from army worms, locusts, hoppers and rodents. One pair bred for seven successive years near Oudtshoorn in 1940, the nest, made of sticks and twigs, being placed high in a dead tree. Repeated spiral flights to a great height are the signal to foregather for migration. They have no voice but rattle their bills. In Afrikaans: Wit Sprinkaanvoël, in Zulu: Ingwamza, in Xhosa: Mokotatsie.

34. Sacred Ibis *Threskiornis aethiopicus* 89 cm R81

Field Identification: Mature birds are white with all the flight feathers tipped with glossy green-black which forms a trailing edge to the wings. The head and neck are bald and black, continuing in a downward curve to the long brown-black bill. In breeding plumage the innermost secondaries and scapulars terminate in glossy violet-blue plumes, underparts tinted with pale gold. Eyes dark brown, long legs black tinted with dark red. Females are similar and young birds are mottled black and white on head and neck and have no plumes.

Distribution: Widely distributed on fresh water, at tidal mud-flats, on farmlands, and on the guano islands. Not a regular migrant, one could say that it is the only resident ibis present throughout the south western Cape.

Notes: A colonial breeder, often with other species such as Egrets, from July to March. The nest is formed from sticks padded with grass. Eggs usually number two to four, of chalky white, with red-brown spots. Food is derived from probing in loose soil or wading in shallow water where water beetles, frogs, and other aquatic insects are found. Grasshoppers, snails, crickets and young birds are also eaten. Utters a harsh croak. In Afrikaans: Skoorsteenveër, in Zulu: um-Xwagele, in Sotho: Leha-langone.

35. Glossy Ibis *Plegadis falcinellus* 71 cm R83

Field Identification: When non-breeding the plumage is a glossy iridescent green with grey below, the head and neck streaked with black and white. During the

breeding season the head, neck, mantle and underparts become a rich glossy chestnut brown, with the wings a spectacular iridescent glossy green shot through with marina and purple. Eyes are brown and the long, thin, curved bill greyish brown; the long legs a dark brownish olive. Females are similar and young birds are a sooty blackish brown. When in flight the legs project slightly beyond the end of the tail.

Distribution: Used to be described as a rare vagrant from the north but in recent years it has become increasingly frequent on the vleis of the south western Cape.

Notes: Found at marshes and on the edges of quiet waterways. Feeds on insects, worms and crustacea. A graceful slender bird with a similarity to the Curlews, appearing black in the distance. Breed from September to January laying two or three bright blue glossy eggs. The nest, made of shredded reeds, is to be found near water in thick reed beds. Not often heard making any sound but a 'kwuk-kwuk-kwuk-kwuk' has been recorded from a bird at a breeding colony. This species breeds regularly at Rondevlei and Berg River. In Afrikaans: Glansende Ibis; in Zulu: in-Kankane.

36. Hadeda *Bostrychia hagedash* 76 cm R84

Field Identification: A fairly large bird, heavier in build and with shorter legs than the glossy Ibis, with a long, thin, downward-curved brown bill coloured a crimson orange along the top. The general colouring is a dull olivy-grey with a metallic pinkish blue on the shoulders and wings. The upper chest is lighter, the eyes dark brown and the legs and feet a dull greyish red. Females are similar and young birds are somewhat duller and have shorter bills.

Distribution: Most prevalent in the more southern parts of the area. Found foraging in small groups of up to about thirty birds in wooded or bushy areas near streams, and sometimes in open veld.

Notes: The Hadeda is readily identifiable by its heavy laborious flight and the silhouette of the broad rounded wings. The feet do not extend beyond the tail feathers in flight. Characteristically they rise up with loud calls when disturbed, usually resettling on nearby trees. Feed on crickets, locusts, beetles, larvae, snails or worms. Breeding takes place from September to December. Nests are formed from a platform of sticks, softened with grass. The place to find them is in trees on the banks of a river. Eggs number three or four and have reddish markings on a pale olive background. The name derives from the sound 'ha-de-da' or 'ha-ha-ha-dahah' emitted when arriving at or departing from the roost. In Afrikaans: Hadeda, in Zulu: in-Kankane, in Xhosa: i-Ngagane.

37. African Spoonbill *Platalea alba* 91 cm R85

Field Identification: Could quite easily be mistaken for a white Egret from a distance, but, once the spoonshaped or spatulate greyish red bill is seen, identification is obvious. Crested at the back of the head and neck, with bare red face, plumage entirely white, eyes pearly grey and long legs red. Sexes alike. Young birds have heads streaked with blackish brown, dusky yellow bills, black feet, and brown tips on primaries. This species is often seen flying in formation, with head and neck extended.

Distribution: Has greatly increased during the last twenty years and is now common, usually seen in small parties wading in marshes or lagoons.
Notes: Often sleeps standing on one leg with bill and head tucked under scapulars. Probe in mud sweeping bill from side to side in the search for food, which is mainly water insects. Locusts are eaten when available. Walk with a fairly slow deliberate tread. Remain separate even though breeding in communities with other birds, the breeding season being from April to December. Flat nests, formed from reeds or water plants, are built in marshes and two or three white eggs, with olivy tan marks at the obtuse end, are laid. The African Spoonbill makes three different sounds, a contented guttural grunt at the nest, a sharp 'kor' in flight and a 'wark-wark' to sound an alarm. In Afrikaans: Lepelaar, in Zulu: in-Xulamasela.

38. Greater Flamingo *Phoenicopterus ruber* 140 cm R86

Field Identification: Unmistakable with its extremely long thin pink legs, white plumage tinged with pink, and thick, pink, curved beak with its terminal third black. Larger than the Lesser Flamingo. Eyes a pale straw colour. A glorious sight in flight, displaying beautiful scarlet and black wings, neck and legs held straight, except when taking off, when the long legs often hang down in a rather ungainly manner. Females are similar and young birds lack the red on wings, are streaked with brown,

and the bill is white tipped with black.

Distribution: Mostly a summer migrant from October to April. They may be very numerous one year, with flocks estimated up to a million birds, while in other years hardly any are to be seen. Frequent at tidal mudflats, vleis, pans and lagoons.

Notes: Often seen standing stamping in shallow water with the neck bent downwards so that the upper mandible is beneath the lower, zig-zagging the head from side to side sifting the disturbed mud through the lamellae of the bill as they feed on plankton. This species will swim if the water is deep and will feed in deep water with head and neck immersed. Food is derived from animal matter, insect larvae, shrimps and molluscs. Breeds irregularly in Southern Africa but in 1960 a breeding colony was discovered in Bredasdorp. Nests are hollowed mounds of mud and there is normally just one white egg. The call is like the 'honk-honk' of domestic geese. In Afrikaans: Groot Flamink.

39. Lesser Flamingo *Phoeniconaias minor* 102 cm R87

Field Identification: Smaller than the Greater Flamingo and with the general plumage tinted more pink, with black flight feathers. Quite often flocks are seen in which all the plumage is of a bright reddish pink – a spectacular and unforgettable sight in flight. Eyes are an orangy red, bill deep red, sometimes appearing black when at a considerable distance, legs red. Females are similar and young birds are light brown.

Distribution: Rather less numerous in the south western Cape than the Greater Flamingo – visitors tending to frequent the more permanent waters.

Notes: This species does not stamp and circle while feeding like the Greater Flamingo, but skim the surface of the water with their bills, food being derived from vegetable matter, especially algae. Nests are a mound of mud formed in shallow water which eventually dries up, leaving the nest on dry land. The voice is like the honk of a goose. In Afrikaans: Klein Flamink.

40. Spurwing Goose *Plectropterus gambensis* 102 cm R88

Field Identification: The name is derived from the large spurs on the shoulder which are put to use when fighting. Identified by its large size, long fairly big neck and general black colouring. The adult male has an iridescent green in the upper black colouring and the amount of white on face and shoulder varies in different individuals. The bill and the patch of bare skin on the head are red, with bare face grey, mottled with white. Legs and feet are fleshy pink, eyes brown. Females are similar but rather duller, young birds have no frontal knob and are brownish.

Distribution: Regularly seen on temporary vleis and huge flocks occur in winter in the Bredasdorp district.

Notes: A shy and wary bird seen congregating in areas next to large expanses of water as well as at streams and rivers where there are water weeds and grass in which to hide. Feed on young plants and grasses. Breeding takes place mainly from September to January and although it is thought that the Spurwing Goose does not breed regularly in the south western Cape, it is probable that it does in the more northern parts of the area and in Bredasdorp. The nest is made from reeds and other vegetation, in holes or dense grass. Eggs number as many as six to twelve and are a glossy ivory. The call is a high-pitched 'ter-whitt' uttered in flight. In Afrikaans: Wildemakou, in Zulu i-Hoye, in Sotho: Letsikhui; in Xhosa: Ihoye.

41. Egyptian Goose *Alopochen aegyptiacus* 71 cm R89

Field Identification: A chestnut ring around the eye as well as a chestnut marking on the white chest will identify this species from the South African Shelduck which it much resembles at a distance. The male is a pale buff with rump and tail black, and

 flight feathers black and white below, white above. Bill light pink, dark tipped, legs pinkish red, eyes varying from orange-brown to crimson. While swimming the general appearance is chestnut and buff but in flight the black primary flight feathers contrast with the white upper side of the wings and the olivy-chestnut inner secondaries. Females are slightly smaller and less bright in colour, and young birds lack the chestnut eye rings and breast patch, being more sooty above and white beneath, with white on the forehead and above the eye.

Distribution: Egyptian Geese will be found throughout the south western Cape wherever there are freshwater vleis, lakes or dams. There has been a noticeable increase in numbers since hunting of them has been curtailed.

Ringed birds have been recovered both in South West Africa and in the Transvaal.

Notes: This species often nests in old nests of other species such as the Hamerkop, in the hollow of a tree, or even in the ledges of a precipice. Males become very aggressive during the breeding season which may be from July to March, but especially during September and October in this area. Eggs number seven to nine, creamy white and fairly glossy, hidden by feathers and down in the nest. Usually found in pairs, but vast flocks can become a pest in the Cape's wheat growing areas where they not only eat new plants but trample them as well. Other food sources are various soft vegetable substances and young grass. Moults after the breeding season. Female birds utter a loud 'honk-honk' and males call in a softer 'haah-haah', sometimes described as a hiss. In Afrikaans: Kolgans, in Xhosa: Ildwe, in Sotho: le-Faloa.

42. South African Shelduck *Tadorna cana* 64 cm R90

Field Identification: Rather similar to the Egyptian Goose but the male, as seen in the photograph, has a grey head and the female a white head, with grey on the back of the head and neck. The female is sometimes mistaken for the Whitefaced Duck unless the male is with her to verify her identification. There is a distinct ringed line of demarcation between the grey colouring of the head and the chestnut of the body, the lower back being deeper chestnut and the upper chest and under belly being somewhat paler. In flight the black primary and tail feathers, white wing coverts and olive green secondaries are clearly evident. Bill and legs black, eyes brown. Young birds are brownish above and white below.

Distribution: Widely distributed throughout the south western Cape, especially on the Peninsula where they are seen on mud banks, sleeping or preening in large flocks, also next to vleis, lakes or dams. It is believed that they are becoming rarer due to the killing of blackbacked jackals which normally feed on the small predators that prey on the eggs of the South African Shelduck.

Notes: A rather shy species which puts to flight readily when disturbed. Occur in large flocks when not breeding and live on various vegetable matter. The male has a deep sonorous call like 'how' or 'honk', uttered at intervals, the female has a higher pitched harsh 'hark', or both may hiss. Breed away from water, usually in antbear holes. Eggs number as many as ten and are a matt white colour. Moulting takes place after the breeding period which is from November to January. In Afrikaans: Bergeend.

43. Cape Shovelor *Anas smithii* 53 cm R94

Field Identification: A fairly large duck with a big spatulate bill which is a dark reddish brown to black in the male bird, as seen in the photograph, and horn coloured in the female. The general colour is a sandy beige background heavily mottled with dark brown markings, the head and neck being finely and rather lightly mottled in

comparison to the heavy marking on the rest of the body. The shoulder feathers are slate blue and the green speculum, edged with white, is seen in flight. The legs and webbed feet are bright yellow, the eyes light yellow. The adult female is darker on the head and the blue on the shoulder is duller than in the male bird. Young birds are similar to the female but pale lemon yellow below.

Distribution: Like the Yellowbilled Duck this species is found throughout the area but is not quite as prolific, though it has greatly increased in recent years. A bird ringed at Rondevlei was recovered in Ovamboland, approximately 1 500 km distant, and one ringed at Barberspan in the Transvaal was found near Bredasdorp.

Notes: Friendly birds mixing with other species except during the breeding period when they remain in pairs. If alarmed they take off almost vertically from the water before flying forwards rapidly. Their flight is probably the fastest of all local ducks. Feeding is 'shovelling' around in the water for aquatic insects and small floating plants. Breeds at any time during the year but mainly from August to October. Nests are to be found in thick clumps of grass containing six to eleven cream coloured eggs. An interesting point is that, although no down is used to line the nest under the eggs, there is a ring of down next to the egg, used to cover it in the absence of the parent bird. The female has a usual ducklike 'quack' and the male has a low guttural call. In Afrikaans: Kaapse Slopeend.

44. African Black Duck *Anas sparsa* 56 cm R95

Field Identification: A plump sooty-black to sooty-brown duck, widely distributed but fairly hard to spot, as they hide in vegetation during the day. There are white markings on the back and tail, and a white band above and below the greenish speculum, underside of wings white. Distinguished from the Yellowbilled Duck by its slate coloured bill with a black central portion and a black line down the middle. eyes brown, legs and webbed feet orange to yellow. The female is similar, young birds browner with underparts a dirty white, spotted with black.

Distribution: To be found in widely distributed areas of the south western Cape in well wooded streams and rivers.

Notes: Inclined to fly very low over the water with wing tips almost touching the surface. Non-gregarious and aggressively territorial. Their colouring acts as a camouflage while they rest during the day in the vegetation, their active time being at dawn and dusk. Feed on insects from rivers, crabs or seed and have developed a liking for acorns, living exclusively on them in some areas. They dive well and will feed with the entire head submerged in the water. The female makes a loud 'quack' and the

male a quiet 'peep'. Breeding takes place from July to February and they often have a permanent nesting site above flood level. Nests are thickly lined with down and may be on driftwood caught in trees at the edge of a river, or on thick matted grass. The creamy buff eggs, numbering five to seven, are covered with down during the absence of the parent bird. In Afrikaans: Swart Eend, in Zulu or Xhosa: Idada.

45. Yellowbilled Duck *Anas undulata* 58 cm R96

Field Identification: Probably the commonest duck in Southern Africa and distinguished from the Black Duck by the yellow bill with its black upper ridge and the dark blackish-brown legs and feet. The general colouring is dark brownish grey mottled all over with narrow white bands edging the plumage, except on the head and neck. In flight the wings are white beneath but brown at the base. The female is similar and young birds are duller in colouring, white beneath, with the breast feathers tinged slightly with pink and a light streak over the eye.

Distribution: Abundant throughout the area though fluctuating in numbers and being most numerous in February. A bird ringed at Barberspan in the Transvaal has been recovered at Rondevlei.

Notes: Flies rapidly, high in the sky, with head held up. Seen in large flocks except when breeding, which is from June to November, with a peak in August. The nest is

constructed from fine grass and lined with down. Eggs number six to twelve yellowish ivory in colour. This species feeds on vegetable matter, grass and seeds. Will put on a 'broken-wing' display to divert attention from its nest of ducklings. After the breeding season there is a flightless moulting period lasting about 36 days. The voice is a loud and raucous quacking. In Afrikaans: Geelbek, in Xhosa: Idada.

46. Cape Teal *Anas capensis* 46 cm R98

Field Identification: A medium sized duck lighter in colour than the Yellowblled or the African Black Duck. The head, neck, chest and underparts are a dirty white, finely marked with blackish brown. The back has bars of blackish-brown and the upper plumage is the same colour narrowly edged with buff. The upper wing coverts are brown and the speculum is white surrounding a shiny green square, clearly seen in flight. The under portion of the wing is dark brown. The bill is rosy pink with black both at the base and tip. Legs and webbed feet yellowish beige, eyes orange. Females similar, young birds duller and smaller.

Distribution: Common in western Cape and vastly increasing in numbers in the past few years. Birds ringed at Rondevlei have been recovered in South West Africa and Mozambique. Will tolerate brak water and are found on lagoons and tidal mud-flats, salt-pans, estuaries and coastal waters.

Notes: When disturbed will fly a short distance and resettle. Feeds on vegetation from its watery surroundings, also insects and seeds, and is to be seen diving and upending for this purpose. The female utters a nasal 'quarrk' and the male utters a high-pitched whistle on the wing. Breed all year round in the south western Cape

and the nest could be under bushes, in rushes or thick grass or in old goose nests. The nest is lined with down and contains six to ten pale cream eggs. In Afrikaans: Teeleendjie.

47. Whitefaced Duck *Dendrocygna viduata* 48 cm R100

Field Identification: The white face is a conspicuous feature, the only other species with a similar feature is the Shelduck but the Whitefaced Duck can be distinguished from that species by the fact that there is no white on the wings. The white face is variable and becomes discoloured before the moult which follows the breeding season. There is also a white patch on the throat contrasting with the black around

the neck and on back of head. The lower neck and upper chest are deep chestnut, the flanks finely barred in black and white, rump, tail, underparts and underside of wings black, upper wings brown with plumage finely edged in buff. Eyes dark brown, bill black with leaden tip, legs and webbed feet lead grey. In flight the wings have a rounded appearance. The female is similar but a little lighter below and young birds are still lighter below, not pure white on face, and markings are paler than in an adult bird.

Distribution: Appear to be moving south from the more northern parts of South Africa and various sightings have been recorded in the south western Cape. In 1979 they were seen at Strandfontein and in 1980 at Princess Vlei.

Notes: Where they are more prevalent they are highly gregarious occurring in flocks on open water. Sleep or preen during the day, feed and fly at night. Live on corms and seeds, as well as molluscs and crustacea found while wading in shallow water. Show alarm by standing tall and then flying off in a slow heavy manner and circling while calling – a clear whistle of three notes like 'sip-sip-sieu'. The nest is a shallow depression lined with a few bits of grass, containing five to twelve creamy white eggs. In Afrikaans: Nonnetjie-eend.

48. Fulvous Whistling Duck *Dendrocygna bicolor* 46 cm R101

Field Identification: A distinct mark of identification is a black line running from the back of the head down the centre nape. Another is that in flight the tail coverts are white. The general colour is light chestnut with an encircling collar of white, finely speckled with black, and white markings on the flanks. The mantle is dusky edged with light chestnut, the rounded wings brown. Legs and feet are bluish slate and extend beyond the tail in flight. Eyes dark brown, bill bluish black.

Distribution: A rare visitor to the area but it has been recorded and has bred on the Cape Peninsula.

Notes: Preens or sleeps during the day becoming active at night. Associates freely with the Yellowbilled Duck. Seeds and corms form the greater part of the diet but

42

crustacea are eaten when wading in shallow water. Flight is slow and sometimes accompanied by a soft whistling 'tsii-ee, tsoo-ee'. A great deal of care is exercised in the construction of nests. Reeds are first of all bent down to form the base and then reeds and rushes are piled thickly on top. Sometimes the nest is lined with down as well. It is usually well hidden in tall grass or bracken, containing from six to twelve buff coloured eggs. In Afrikaans: Fluit-eend.

49. Southern Pochard *Netta erythrophthalma* 51 cm R102

Field Identification: A medium sized duck which looks almost black in the distance but which on closer inspection is fairly colourful. The male is dark brown on the head, crown and nape, with chestnut on sides of head and neck. The back, tail and flight feathers are brown and there is a mottled sandy colouring on mantle, upper

chest and underparts with lower chest plain tawny. A broad single white bar is to be seen on the wing plumage. The eye varies from orange to blood red, the bill is very pale slate blue, legs and webbed feet dark grey. The female has a greyer bill with an edging of white feathers at the base. The general colouring is slightly lighter than that of the male, and there is a white mark from the eye down the side of the neck. Ducklings are brown above and yellow on underparts.
Distribution: Present in fluctuating numbers throughout the year though virtually absent in May. Regularly seen on permanent vleis with males outnumbering females.
Notes: Favour deep water and will remain in the centre of a wide stretch sitting low in the water with the tail characteristically submerged. Will run along the surface of the water when alarmed before getting airborne and when in flight the domed forehead and thin neck in silhouette assist identification. Breeding time in the Cape is from August to December. The nest, containing either a sparse amount of down or none at all, is built in a dry place in the reeds above water. Eggs number between six and thirteen, creamy buff and pitted. Feed mainly on seeds and aquatic vegetation. The female utters a short 'quarrk' and the male either a nasal 'whreeooorrr' or 'par-ah-ah'. In Afrikaans: Bruin Eend.

50. Maccoa Duck *Oxyura maccoa* 46 cm R103

Field Identification: The male has a black head and nape, with upper parts bright chestnut, wings brown and underparts mottled brown and tawny. One photograph shows the male during a courting display. The female, as seen on the nest, is dark brownish grey with a rather speckled black head, and with an indistinct lightish stripe from the side of the bill along the side of the face. Chin and throat speckled whitish, back and chest speckled with chestnut on the dark background. Eyes are

♀

dark brown. The male has a bill varying from bright blue to black, and that of the female is dark greyish brown. Legs and webbed feet lead colour. Ducklings are blackish brown above and lighter below.

Distribution: Found on dams, lakes or almost any quiet waters. They may be locally common for a few years and apparently resident, and then disappear completely.

They remain rather rare and can be completely absent from seemingly suitable stretches of water.

Notes: Essentially a diving duck, not keen to fly, and taking some time to rise, splashing the surface of the water before taking off. When intimidated this species may become almost totally submerged, with the tail held perpendicularly or submerged as well. The call is a soft 'purr'. Live on seeds, algae, water beetles and roots. Thought to use the nests of other birds such as the Coot or the Great Crested Grebe, but will also build its own nest of reeds. Will be found in family parties or in pairs during the breeding season, which could be at any time of the year, but especially in November and December. Eggs vary from four to twelve and are a pale bluish white colour. In Afrikaans: Makou-eend.

51. Secretarybird *Sagittarius serpentarius* 150 cm R105

Field Identification: Usually seen striding around open country and immediately identifiable by the multiple crest of grey, black-tipped feathers on the back of the head, which resemble the feathers of the old-fashioned quill sticking up, when, in days gone by, a secretary put the quill behind his ear – hence the derivation of the name. The general colouring is medium grey above, with lower plumage black. A wide black band edges the wings which is very evident in flight. The eagle-type bill is bluish white and bare orange skin surrounds the brown eye. Long pink eggs covered with black tibia plumage half way down give a trouser-like effect. The female is slightly smaller and nestlings are generally duller in colour.

Distribution: Widely but sparingly distributed in open country, chiefly on the flats.
Notes: A strong flier nesting on the tops of trees despite its terrestrial habits. The strong legs and feet are used to kill its prey which consists of reptiles, small animals and snakes. This bird of prey can run very fast, with wings partly spread, when pursued. Roosts at night in nests, even during the non-breeding season. Breeds August

to October making a nest of sticks just below the top of a low tree and quite difficult to see. Eggs number two or three and are white. The voice is a deep frog-like croak and a high-pitched call when flying. In Afrikaans: Sekretarisvoël, in Xhosa: i-Nxamxosi, in Zulu: i-Ntungonono, in Sotho: Mamalangoane, in Shona: Wata.

52. Cape Vulture *Gyps coprotheres* 110 cm R106

Field Identification: The lightest in colour of all the vultures with upper parts off-white, ruff at base of neck palest beige and underparts creamy white. The head and neck have a bluish grey appearance with hair-like feathers running from the beak

over the eye area and down to the neck, which has a sparse offwhite down. The primaries and tail are black, secondaries ash-brown, bill curved and powerful – for tearing flesh from carcasses. Females are similar and young birds are browner in colour.

Distribution: In past years these birds of prey were plentiful in the south western Cape but their numbers have been greatly depleted due to inadvertent poisoning from eating poisoned bait intended for jackals. Many have died by electrocution on power lines. Today they are seen mostly in the northern and eastern sections and there is a breeding colony on the Potberg in the extreme south eastern area.

Notes: The Cape Vulture is a scavenging bird of prey with very keen eyesight, sighting carcasses from a great height. The stomach of the dead animal is torn open and these vultures eat the softer parts from within the body, fighting each other with wings partly outstretched, uttering a grating cry. Breeding time is from May to November and takes place in communities high up on the ledges of precipices in the mountains. Sheets of white droppings on rocks below indicate their presence. Nests vary from being carefully constructed and lined with vegetation, to nothing but a bare ledge where one pure white egg is laid. In Afrikaans: Krans-aasvoël, in Sotho: le-Tlaka.

53. Peregrine *Falco peregrinus* 34–38 cm R113

Field Identification: The females of this species are larger than the males but in other respects the sexes appear similar. Distinguished from the Lanner by the blackish crown and heavier barring below. Upper parts blackish, extending over sides of face beneath the dark brown eye, which has a yellow surround. The throat and sides of neck are whitish with a chestnut tint, and lower parts heavily barred with black. Bill bluish grey and dark tipped, cere and legs yellow. Young birds brownish above and heavily streaked below.

Distribution: Usually found in mountainous or hilly terrain but becoming rarer in the area.

Notes: Has a fast wingbeat, which is a distinguishing characteristic in flight when it is impossible to see the colour of the crown in order to distinguish this species from the Lanner. Found singly or in pairs, usually perched on a high rock or tree. A truly bold and dashing falcon which swoops on its prey at incredible speed with its wings folded. This is called 'stooping' and the Peregrine will strike its victim with its claws at this tremendous speed and with the hind claw strike its victim's head from its body. Should the blow be unsuccessful it will climb steeply once more and descend again to its kill. Lives on birds, especially doves and pigeons. Nests on cliffs where the nest is nothing but a shallow scrape, or occasionally in the nests of other birds in trees. Three eggs, white, but heavily marked with reddish, are laid during the period from July to October. In Afrikaans: Slegvalk.

54. Lanner *Falco biarmicus* 40–45 cm R114

Field Identification: At all ages the crown is rufous, but the forehead is dark, and, viewed from the front, as in the photograph, one might mistake this species for the Peregrine, but a further distinguishing feature is much less heavy barring on the underparts. As in the previous species the female is similar but larger than the male. Mantle and wings are blackish, tail feathers grey with darker bars. Chin, throat and upper chest light pinkish grey, lower belly and flanks barred with blackish grey. In flight the Lanner appears longer in body and with broader wings than the Peregrine, and the tail feathers are fan-shaped, not straight. The bill is horn with a blue tip, skin around the brown eyes yellow, legs yellow.

Distribution: Rare in the south western Cape. Its normal habitat is in fairly dry mountainous terrain or in open country, bit it occasionally comes into small towns, and is less dependent on cliffs for breeding purposes.

Notes: This species is trained for falconry. Lives on Rock Pigeons, doves, and various waders, ducks, francolins and finches, as well as locusts, insects and reptiles. The wingbeat is relatively slow and the flight pattern takes the form of active flight followed by short glides. The call is a loud sharp 'chack-chack-chack', a piercing

scream followed by a 'kweep', or a soft 'kek-kek-kek' at the nest. Old crow or vulture nests are sometimes used, or the nest may be placed on a cliff ledge. Three or four eggs are laid which are white, covered with red, yellow and purply brown blotches. In Afrikaans: Edelvalk, in xhosa: Ukhetshe, in Sotho: Phakoe.

55. Common Kestrel *Falco tinnunculus* 32 cm R123

Field Identification: Mainly a golden cinnamon colour lightly speckled with streaks of black. The adult male has head and nape a darkish slate blue while the female has these areas in dark grey. Females have tail feathers barred but lose barring when old. Young birds have crown rufous and tails barred like the female. Eyes dark brown, bills pinkish around the nostrils and bluish grey towards the curved tip, legs pinkish yellow.

Distribution: Throughout the south western Cape and found anywhere, but favours hilly or mountainous regions and seldom strays from its familiar haunts.

Notes: Seen most often sitting in pairs on telegraph poles – a vantage point to watch for prey – or characteristically hovering. Occasionally enters town and nests on buildings. Feeds on mice and other small mammals, lizards, insects and occasionally birds. Will feed in flight, holding its prey with its claws. Prefers nesting on ledges. Breeding takes place from August to October when four eggs are laid of a blotchy red colour. The call is a plaintive 'kee-kee', an alarm call, 'kirrriie' and a shrill 'kek,kek-,kek,'. In Afrikaans: Rooivalkie, in Sotho: Seotsanyana, in Xhosa: Utebetebana, in Zulu: u-Matebeni.

56. Lesser Kestrel *Falco naumanni* 28−30 cm R125

Field Identification: The unspotted chestnut back, lighter underparts and grey-blue wing-coverts and secondaries readily distinguish the male Lesser Kestrel from other Kestrels. The photograph of the male shows clearly the top of head, nape, rump and upper tail-coverts dove grey. Underparts are light buff and underside of wings whitish, eyes brown, bill blue-grey, cere and legs yellowish, and at all ages and in both sexes the claws are very light almost whitish. The female appears larger than the male, light brown above streaked with black, rump grey, buff to lightish chestnut below with light black streaks, tail barred rufous above and barred greyish below with a black subterminal band. Young birds resemble the female.

♀

Distribution: A non-breeding migrant from Europe and Asia which is common between Caledon and Mossel Bay and in the south eastern Karoo. Prefers open grassveld.

Notes: Forages for insects in the open veld during the day and is commonly seen perched on a post or telegraph wire. Gather in large flocks to roost at night in large trees, which are often only to be found in towns, where they can become quite a nuisance soiling parks and gardens with their droppings. In addition to eating insects they live on locusts when available and are protected by law due to their usefulness. The call is a high pitched rattling 'tirr-tirr-tirr'. Arrive in late October and remain during the summer months departing during the first week in March in the south west Cape. In Afrikaans: Klein Rooivalkie.

57. Yellowbilled Kite *Milvus migrans* 55 cm R129

Field Identification: The general appearance, including the head is brown, and a distinguishing feature is the yellow hooked bill. In flight the long tail is forked and the long black wings bend back at the carpal joint. Eyes brown, cere and legs yellow. The female resembles the male and young birds do not have forked tails, the bill is brown and the general colour is lighter.

Distribution: Present throughout southern Africa, but in the south western Cape it is uncommon on the Peninsula, becoming progressively commoner towards the northern areas, and breeding in some numbers along the Berg and Olifants Rivers. Fairly common in the Swartland.

Notes: In flight the head is pulled back and this kite has an unusual habit of twisting its tail from one side to the other as it changes its direction. Sometimes seen feeding on food held in its talons while flying high in the sky. The picture shows a Yellowbilled Kite with its prey in the form of a dead rabbit, but this species lives on a variety of rats, lizards, shrews, frogs, small birds, snails, insects and harvester ter-

mites as well. Very valuable to the south western Cape area as it eats great numbers of destructive mole rats. Often seen on the ground and usually singly. The call is a grating 'chew,chi, chi,chi' at the nest, or a plaintive 'kleeeuw' ending in a trill. Breeding takes place from September to December, the nest, usually placed high up in a tree being a platform of sticks lined with scraps of cloth or wool and containing two or three white eggs with brown markings. In Afrikaans: Geelbekwou, in Xhosa: u-Tloyile, in Sotho: Mankloli, in Zulu: i-Nkoinyana.

58. Blackshouldered Kite *Elanus caeruleus* 30 cm R130

Field Identification: Probably the most numerous bird of prey in the area. Fairly small with a general grey colouring, black shoulder plumage, white head, neck, throat, chest and underparts. The flight feathers are black, the shortish tail grey, bill greyish black, legs and claws yellow, eyes bright red. The female is similar and young birds are brown on the sides of the neck and breast.

Distribution: Found in open country especially in coastal Macchia as well as throughout the south western Cape.

Notes: Often seen perched on telegraph poles with wing tips drooping below the tail feathers. In flight this species rather resembles a gull. Inclined to hover while seeking out its prey and to stop several times in its descent before swooping down with feet extended. Breeds during the spring with nests high up in tall trees, sometimes using vacated nests. Eggs number three or four with one end streaked with brown.

Live on mice, lizards, locusts and a variety of insects, rarely attacking other birds. Usually seen singly or in pairs during the day but will gather in flocks up to about fifty in number to roost at night. The call is a clear, loud, 'fwee'. In Afrikaans: Blouvalkie, in Sotho: Matlakokoane, in Xhosa: Umdlampuku.

59. Black Eagle *Aquila verreauxii* 84 cm R133
(Pictured overleaf)

Field Identification: A magnificent bird, all black with a white V-shaped marking on the back and a white rump. Black feathers extend down legs to base of yellow toes. In flight the inner web of the primaries shows white, and the wings are spear-shaped with characteristic narrowness at the base. Sexes are alike and young birds are tawny brown. Eyes brown, bill horn, cere and claws yellow.
Distribution: Seen regularly in the mountainous areas of the south western Cape and it is thought that there are three pairs resident on the Peninsula mountains.
Notes: Wonderful to watch in flight, soaring, climbing vertically or making loops after a dive. Their method of hunting is usually to surprise prey by flying fast among the cliffs and ridges and attacking dassies, small antelope, young baboons or guinea-fowl. The large nest is constructed usually on a cliff ledge, but sometimes in a tree, almost always very inaccessible. Eggs are laid between March and July. If two eggs are laid it is usual for only one eagle to survive as one usually kills the other. The Black Eagle makes a loud yelping cry. In Afrikaans: Witkruis-arend, in Sotho: Ntsu, in Zulu and Xhosa: n-Kozi.

60. Booted Eagle *Hieraaëtus pennatus* 50 cm R139

Field Identification: There are two types of these birds occurring in two colour phases. The one photographed at the nest is white below, the other type is dark brown below, the white variety being the more common. The dark variety is similar to Wahlberg's Eagle but smaller. In flight the pale bird appears all white from beneath, with outstretched wings edged with greyish black, and under-wing coverts spotted. The dark bird appears all black in flight from beneath, with tail feathers grey. The pale bird has white feathers down to the base of its yellow toes, while those on the dark bird are dark buff. Upper parts are mottled light brown, dark brown and white, eyes golden hazel, but brown in young birds, bill greyish black, cere and claws yellow.

Distribution: A migrant breeding in Europe and Asia, visiting the Cape in the summer months, however breeding has been recorded near Clanwilliam at Niewoudtville in the Sewe Weeks Poort and at Ceres. The picture shows a breeding bird with a tiny white nestling photographed at Sewe Weeks Poort.

Notes: The Booted Eagle swoops out of trees at great speed to kill its prey – usually ground birds, small animals and poultry. A bold and rapacious species. The call is a shrill descending 'kee'. the nest is usually found in a tree growing on a kranz and containing two white eggs. In Afrikaans: Dwergarend.

61. Martial Eagle *Polemaëtus bellicosus* 83 cm R142

Field Identification: A large powerful bird distinguishable from the Blackbreasted Snake Eagle by its white breast, spotted with brown, and its feathered legs. Head, neck, upper chest and flight feathers are ash brown, eyes yellow, brown in young, bill greyish black. The female is much larger than the male and immature birds have throat, chest and underparts white, lacking the distinctive spots of adult birds. Cere grey, legs bluish white. One photograph shows female and nestling, the other shows the adult male.

Distribution: Found throughout southern Africa but largely exterminated in the south western Cape where it used to be generally distributed in the drier parts. Still

found in the wilder and more remote mountainous areas. Has bred in the Potberg.
Notes: The Martial Eagle is protected in many areas for its great usefulness in curbing the dassie plague and limiting the hare population. It flies at a considerable height spying out the land for its prey which it strikes powerfully and kills instantly.

Ground-squirrels, game-birds, monkeys, small antelope, snakes and rodents also form part of its food. The breeding season is from April to July, the nest being constructed by the female with sticks supplied by the male. Nests are used year after year and become huge, as can be seen in the picture, measuring as much as two metres across, perhaps as high as sixty metres up in a large tree. One or two eggs are laid, white in colour sparsely speckled with brown and slate. The call is a long 'kloo-ee-kloo-ee-kloo-ee' and an occasional low 'gwolp'. In Afrikaans: Breëkop-arend, in Xhosa: Ukhozi.

62. Blackbreasted Snake Eagle *Circaetus gallicus* 67 cm R146

Field Identification: Smaller than the Martial Eagle with scaled, unfeathered legs of a dirty white colour, breast unspotted, but in general appearance very similar. Head, back of neck, upper chest and flight feathers brown, with a white patch at the throat and chest white. Eyes yellow, bill black. The female is a little smaller and immature birds are tawny brown above and a mottled lighter tawny shade below.
Distribution: Seen on rare occasions in Hottentots Holland on the mountain peaks. There is an old specimen from the Malmesbury area to be seen in the South African Museum in Cape Town. The Blackbreasted Snake Eagle avoids heavily forested areas and is still to be found in the drier parts of the Karoo.
Notes: Usually seen watching the ground from a vantage point such as a tall tree or a telegraph pole, or soaring at a fair height, sometimes hovering like a kestrel. Lives on small mammals and lizards but mainly on snakes which it often swallows in flight. It breeds at various times throughout the year laying one rather large white egg found in a fairly small nest four to seven metres high in a tree. Utters a loud shriek while in flight. In Afrikaans: Swartbors-slangarend.

63. Fish Eagle *Haliaeetus vocifer* 73 cm R149

Field Identification: A beautiful bird with head, neck and chest white, underparts deep chestnut and flight feathers black, tipped with chestnut. Young birds have a mottled appearance with underparts a blackish brown. The hooked beak is blackish and the dark chestnut plumage extends down the legs to the powerful claws. Cere and claws are yellowish, grey in young birds.

Distribution: Throughout the south western Cape and found on rivers, lakes, dams, estuaries and even the open seashore – in fact wherever fish are to be caught.

Notes: Found most often in pairs in the vicinity of trees near rivers and large vleis. Lives mainly on stranded and dead fish washed up on a bank but will also swoop on fish swimming in the water, usually checking the swoop before hitting the water but some-

56

times going right under to secure its prey. Will also rob other fish-eating birds and has been seen to kill a heron and a coot. The call is one of the characteristic sounds of Africa and is a loud yelping 'kow kow, kowkowkow' uttered on the wing with the head thrown back. Breeds during the winter months from May to August, laying two rough white eggs in a large nest of sticks, usually lodged in a bush. In Afrikaans: Visarend, in Zulu: i-Nkwazi, in Xhosa: Unomakhwezana.

64. Jackal Buzzard *Buteo rufofuscus* 44 – 53 cm R152

Field Identification: Adult birds are black above with a chestnut tail having a black bar near its tip. Individual birds sometimes have a white chin and throat. Chest chestnut and underparts nearly black or a mixture of chestnut and black. Primaries are black with basal half grey, secondaries light grey barred with black. Thigh plumage dark with lighter streaks, legs and cere yellowish, eyes brown, bill greyish horn. Young birds are brown above with black on forehead, nape and mantle, chestnut below with darker streaks. Chicks are a lighter grey on head and neck as seen in the picture.

Distribution: Resident and common except in the Strandveld, favouring the Cape Fynbos; present in the mountains and into neighbouring plains.
Notes: The name derives from the fact that the call is said to resemble a jackal cry. Seen perching on a vantage point or soaring high overhead. Will eat dead animals killed on the road and will occasionally kill chickens, the usual food being derived from reptiles, insects and various mammals. Nests on a ledge in a precipice, as can be seen in the picture, or in bushes growing on the cliffs. Two white eggs marked with reddish speckles are laid during the period from June to October. In Afrikaans: Jakkalsvoël, in Xhosa or Zulu: Indlandlokazi, in Sotho: Khayoane.

65. Steppe Buzzard *Buteo buteo* 45 – 50 cm R154

Field Identification: Variable in plumage with three distinct phases but in flight all show whitish underwing with rufous coverts and dark trailing edge. Dark brown on upper parts, mixed with chestnut on mantle and back, and mixed with buff on head, neck and chest. Tail feathers are variable either light or dark and barred. Eyes brown, bill black, cere and legs yellow. Young birds are brown above, buff below, with streaks. Sexes alike.

Distribution: A non-breeding migrant from the Palaearctic. Arrives in the Peninsula area towards the end of October, remaining for the summer months and leaving again in March. Ringed birds have been recovered in Russia 12,000 kms distant and in Iraq. A breeding pair, resembling a phase of this species, was found at Constantia in 1960 and in 1961, and in Hottentots Holland in 1980. Favours open woodland and even dry semi-desert areas.

Notes: Feeds on lizards, frogs, insects, rats, mice, chameleons and some birds. Is seen watching for insects or other prey from a fence, a tree or a lamp-post. It is usually rather quiet while visiting this country during the non-breeding season but its call is a mewing 'kee-you, kee-you'. In Afrikaans: Bruin Jakkalsvoël, in Xhosa: Isanxha or u-Magoloda, in Sotho: Nkholi.

66. Mountain buzzard *Buteo tachardus* 45 cm R155

Field Identification: Distinguished from the Steppe Buzzard by a relatively unmarked white band across the lower chest. Upper parts brown mottled with chestnut, chin, throat and chest blotched with brown on white, mainly higher up; lower belly and underparts mixed white and chestnut. Thighs dark, appearing blackish in flight. Tail barred with dark brown on lighter ground and a blackish subterminal band, tipped narrowly with offwhite. eyes golden brown, bill blackish, cere and legs yellow. Sexes are similar and young birds have light biscuit coloured eyes during their first year.

Distribution: Previously present only eastwards from the George and Knysna area and still rare in the south western Cape but increasing. A resident species now breeding in the area, frequenting forested mountainous areas.

Notes: Seen quietly perched on a fence pole or a dead tree, often in plantations of exotics, or soaring high overhead. Lives on frogs and lizards and the call is a piercing 'keeee-o' or 'keeee'. As can be seen in the photograph the nest is a large structure of sticks placed in a tree from about nine to fifteen metres from the ground. Two white eggs are laid. The breeding period is in spring, from September to October. In Afrikaans: Berg-jakkalsvoël.

67. Redbreasted Sparrowhawk
Accipiter rufiventris 33 – 40 cm R156

Field Identification: Slate grey above with a slight brownish wash, chin and throat white, sides of face, chest and underparts tawny finely barred with rufous, giving the characteristic red chest present in the adult bird. Intermediate plumage may appear barred with rufous on white below. Flight feathers dusky, tail widely barred in black and grey with light tip. Thighs chestnut, cere and legs yellow, eyes yellow, bill black. Young birds are streaked on chest and barred on breast.
Distribution: Resident and fairly common in wooded country. Found in copses of tall trees in the Karoo.
Notes: The characteristic flight of the Redbreasted Sparrowhawk is at great speed through thick cover where, relying on the element of surprise, it catches its prey, mainly small birds: Will also take young poultry and feeds on termites and insects as well. The alarm call is a strident 'chek-chek-chek-chek' and during the breeding season, from September to December in the south western Cape, pairs will be seen circling high over trees calling loudly during courtship. The nest is made from sticks, usually placed in a tree, and containing two to four white eggs heavily blotched at the larger end with shades of brown. In Afrikaans: Rooibors-sperwer, in Xhosa: Ukhetshana, in Zulu: u-Mhloile.

68. Pale Chanting Goshawk *Melierax canorus* 53 – 63 cm R165

Field Identification: Grey on head neck and chest, slightly lighter on mantle and wing plumage, rump white, central tail feathers plain grey, outer tail feathers barred. The white secondaries are clearly seen in flight. Thighs, lower belly and underparts finely barred in grey and white. Cere and base of bill orange to brick red, legs red, eyes dark reddish brown. The sexes are similar and young birds are greyish brown above, streaked and barred below with yellow legs and yellowy green eyes.

Distribution: Is not present in the Peninsula. A Karoo species, probably resident in the northern areas of the south western Cape and in parts of the Breede River valley. Those found further south are stragglers.

Notes: Has a gull-like appearance in flight and inhabits mountainous or open country and desert. Often seen perched on telegraph poles or on the highest point of tall trees looking for small weak animals, lizards or insects, mainly taken from the ground. Has a dipping display flight during the courting period when it mounts to a considerable height at dawn, uttering a full clear melodic call. The alarm call is a shrill 'whee' and a 'kek-kek'. Breeding takes place in the winter months from June to August the nest being placed on top of a bush, thorn-tree or telegraph pole and lined with dung, wool and hair. One or two bluish white eggs are laid. In Afrikaans: Groot Witvalk.

69. African Marsh Harrier *Circus ranivorus* 47 cm R167

Field Identification: The Marsh Harrier is deep chestnut and when young has a distinctive white band across the chest. There is a pale patch at the shoulder in flight. Fairly dark brown above with light flecks, flight feathers are dark ash brown barred with black, under wing-coverts checkered chestnut and white. Tail barred, upper

tail-coverts pale chestnut. Male and female are similar, the small hooked beak is black, eyes, cere and legs yellowish. Young birds are blackish brown with pale chestnut markings although some individual birds are plain dark brown all over. Nestlings are offwhite with blackish wing plumage as seen in the photograph.

Distribution: Appears to have declined in numbers in the south western Cape in recent years but is still fairly common in the vicinity of vleis and large marshes.

Notes: This species is the common harrier seen flying low over marsh lands with laboured flight, rarely landing except to pounce on its prey. Has a characteristic backward somersault and sudden pounding fall when young birds, rats or frogs which comprise the diet, are spotted. Breeds in the south western Cape from August to December, nesting in the marshes and making nests from sticks, rushes and reeds. Eggs number three to five and are a blue-tinged white. The call is a mewing cry. In Afrikaans: Paddavreter, in Sotho: Mankholi.

70. Black Harrier *Circus maurus* 53 cm R169

Field Identification: Mainly black in appearance with primary wings edged with silvery grey and rump white. In flight particularly the black tail, with whitish grey bands and white tip, is clearly evident. Blackish brown below, sparsely spotted with white. The hooked bill, below the yellow cere, is black, the legs yellowish brown, eyes yellow. Females are similar but young birds are brown above with beige chest and underparts speckled with brown, light beige around the eyes, and with tail and wings having similar markings to those of adult birds. Nestlings are shown in the photograph.

Distribution: No longer do Black Harriers frequent only the old haunts of previous records, for they are now to be seen in many districts, favouring areas near dams, rivers and vleis, but in drier surroundings than those inhabited by the Marsh Harrier.

Notes: Once almost extinct but recently becoming far more common and widespread, usually seen soaring very high over the breeding territory. Breeding time is from September to October when a nest is built from dry sticks and reeds lined with softer material like bits of wool or hair. Eggs number three to five and are white or white with dark brown markings. Feeds on small frogs, lizards, rodents or baby birds. Has a shrill strident cry. In Afrikaans: Witkruis-valk.

71. Gymnogene *Polyboroides typus* 66 cm R171

Field Identification: The bare, narrow, yellow face, long yellow legs and a broad whitish bar across the long black tail identify the Gymnogene. All young birds show white at the base of the feathers when ruffled but there are two distinct phases of plumage, the first being almost uniform brown and the second being mixed with lighter chestnut and having white, flecked with chestnut, on throat and chest, underparts lightish chestnut streaked with brownish. The mature adult is grey above and on throat and chest, with underparts barred with black and white. The feathers round the nape stand out like a ruff and when breeding the yellow cheeks are reddish. Eyes dark brown, cere yellow, bill black. Females resemble the male.

Distribution: Regular in the Cedarberg and northern areas and recorded as being resident for two years in the Lourensford Valley, Somerset West; elsewhere in the south western Cape it is regarded as a vagrant. Favours parklike treed grasslands.

Notes: The flight pattern has repeated upward flights followed by steep downward swoops accompanied by a thin screaming 'peeeeeee'. Pokes in the cracks and crevices of trees for lizards, young birds and insects while clinging to the bark and flapping its wings. Also feeds on snakes, bats, palm-nut husks and frogs, and is prone to raid weavers' nest for the eggs. During courtship the Gymnogene has a display flight, flying in circles with a very fast wing-beat and uttering a shrill call. The photograph illustrates the typical hawk-type nest in the fork of a large tree, although occasionally the nest is found in the crevice of a cliff. Two white eggs streaked with yellow and brown will be found from September to December. In Afrikaans: Gymnogene.

72. Osprey *Pandion haliaetus* 63 cm R172

Field Identification: The head and ruffed nape are whitish with a wide greyish brown line through the eye and down the side of the neck. The throat is white with spotted brown on upper chest, underparts pale greyish white. The dark slate tips to the wings form a dark trailing edge in flight as seen in the photograph. Upper parts are a dark ashy brown, eyes yellow, curved bill black, cere blue-grey, feathered legs slate below. Females are similar and young birds have the crown streaked and upper plumage edged with buff.

Distribution: A summer visitor to the coast and to the vleis and rivers in the area. The Osprey has been recorded breeding near the mouth of the Berg River, but is very rare.

Notes: Seen perched on a tree overhanging water or when fishing for food has intermittent spells of flapping flight followed by gliding. Swoops down to catch a fish in its very strong talons and will then carry it to a perch. Feeds only on fish. The call is a descending 'tschip-tschip-tschip' and a 'chick-chick'. A migratory species. Eggs number two or three variably marked with red and yellowish brown. In Afrikaans: Visvalk.

73. Greywinged Francolin *Francolinus africanus* 33 cm R176

Field Identification: Upper wing coverts greyish and flight feathers also greyish barred with tawny beige. The head is mottled black and tawny with chestnut streaks down side of neck, throat mottled grey and white. Generally mottled chestnut, tawny beige, black and white with blackish tail barred with beige. The bill is dark grey, legs a dirty yellow, eyes brown. The female is not spurred and young birds have a generally duller colour.

Distribution: Found mainly in the Strandveld and coastal Renosterbosveld where it inhabits indigenous bush.

Notes: These partridges are usually found in large coveys and when disturbed rise en masse from a typical grassy patch; with loud squealing notes to disappear over a nearby hilltop or convenient promintory. Feed on insects, seeds and bulbs. Breed from August to October in the Cape, nesting in grassy areas and laying about six yellowish brown eggs. Typically in the early morning and at sundown their call 'squea-keeoo' can be heard. In Afrikaans: Bergpatrys, in Zulu: in-Tendele, in Sotho: Khuale.

74. Cape Francolin *Francolinus capensis* 42 cm R181

Field Identification: A large bird with a dark mottled earth-brown and white appearance, the dark plumage having thin white edges. There are broad white stripes on the belly, eyes reddish brown, bill dark greyish horn above, red below, legs dull yellow. The female is similar but does not have spurs unless very old.

Distribution: Common throughout the south western Cape in thick cover, tree-lined river banks and coastal Macchia.

Notes: The Cape Francolin is confined in Southern Africa to the south western area and is usually found in family groups sheltering in areas described above. This species becomes quite tame around farm houses. Feeds on insects, berries, bulbs and

seeds. Makes a loud crowing cackle at sunrise and sunset. Breeds from September to December, laying six to eight eggs of a pale or purplish pink, found in a nest under a bush during the months from September to December. In Afrikaans: Kaapse Fisant.

75. Helmeted Guineafowl *Numida meleagris* 58 cm R192

Field Identification: This species is the only Guineafowl in Southern Africa with a casque on the head. The general colouring for both sexes is black spotted with white, giving a mottled grey appearance at a distance. The tip of the casque is horn coloured, the base and the bony part of the head being a brownish red, the penduline wattles blue tipped with red. The sides of the face and neck are turquoise, sparsely spotted with black plumage which forms a slight tuft on the nape. The throat is deep blue. The thick curved bill is red at the base, horn at the tip and the legs and feet dark horn to blackish, eyes brown. Immature birds are more brown, have shorter black casques, and the feathers on the neck are streaked with white.

Distribution: Common in the south western Cape having been introduced into this area before 1900 and valued in the control of weeds and insects in vineyards and orchards. A regular species in coastal Renoster-bosveld, in wooded country and grassland in the proximity of water.

Notes: This species 'runs' a great deal but will fly into trees to escape when chased by dogs. Particularly noisy when about to roost making a loud repeated 'cher-cheng, cher-cheng', the alarm call being a noisy 'kek,kek'. Feed on weeds, insects, bulbs, snails, ticks and wireworms. Breeding takes place from October to March and at this time the flocks pair off, each pair selecting its own area for breeding, and spending much time chasing off any other guineafowl that may encroach. The nest is a shallow scraping under a bush and the clutch numbers six to eight, the eggs having remarkably thick shells of a yellowish hue. Chicks are ready to follow the adults within five hours of hatching and, if disturbed or scattered by a predator, are called together again with a piping whistle. In Afrikaans: Tarentaal, in Sotho: Khaka.

76. Cape Rail *Rallus caerulescens* 38 cm R197

Field Identification: Not an easy bird to spot as it spends much time hidden in reeds and marshy vegetation. The upper parts are a rich brown with face, neck and upper chest grey, underparts barred in a distinct black and white. The long pointed bill is deep red as are the eyes, legs and feet. Females are similar and young birds are sooty brown with throat and centre of chest whitish.

Distribution: Has been recorded from the Black River and Velddrif in summer, Verloren Vlei in spring and Langebaan Lagoon at both seasons. Is present throughout the south western Cape but due to the circumstances of its surroundings, as previously described, it is not often seen and recorded.

Notes: In flight the white under tail-coverts are to be seen, and it will be noted that the long red legs seem to dangle. When venturing into more open muddy areas it will be seen to have jerky movements. The nest is hidden in vegetation above the water and constructed from reeds and blades of rush. Eggs number three to six with red-brown and slate speckles on a cream background, more heavily marked at the thick end. The Cape Rail feeds on tiny water creatures, insects, worms and crabs. Sounds both a low almost growling note, as well as a high-pitched 'Creeeea' followed rapidly by a strident 'crak,crak,crak'. In Afrikaans: Riethaantjie.

77. Baillon's Crake *Porzan pusilla* 18 cm R202

Field Identification: A small Crake rather like the much larger African Crake which inhabits the more north easterly portions of Southern Africa. The crown, nape, mantle and back are a browny chestnut, mottled with black and lightly marked with white. The throat is light, the lower parts slate, and the lower flanks and under tail-coverts barred in black and white. Eyes red, short bill greenish grey, culmen black and legs olivy grey. Females are light brown below and have a white throat. Young birds are barred with brown on chest.

Distribution: An inhabitant of marshes known to have bred near Paarl and at Swartklip. Favours areas where the vegetation is short and is seen running through the grass like a rodent.

Notes: A nervous, skulking species which when disturbed will jerk its tail up and down and its head back and forth, with each step. When flushed from its surroundings it will fly a short distance and dive for cover in the vegetation once again. Protects its eggs, usually numbering four to six in a buff colour over-marked with olive, by placing the nest in short grass and curling rushes over it. Food is derived from plants, seeds and insects. Calls are a low 'quick-quick' and a husky drawn out 'chrrr'. In Afrikaans: Kleinste Riethaantjie, in Xhosa: Isizinzi, in Zulu: isi-Zinze.

78. Black Crake *Amaurornis flavirostris* 22 cm R203

Field Identification: A dramatically coloured bird with its glossy black plumage brilliant red eyes and bright yellow bill. The long legs and elongated claws are red. The female is the same and immature birds are olivy-brown above with white on throat, the white-tipped bill is black and the legs brownish.

Distribution: Common in marshes and resident in the swampy areas and reed beds of the south western Cape.

Notes: Cocks its tail and from a distance looks rather like a bantam as it emerges from the reeds and water plants under which it shelters. Runs a great deal and is quite reluctant to fly but on taking off will fly with a rapid wing action close to the surface of the water. Usually seen in pairs or very small groups. Breeds from September to December constructing the nest from grass and reeds and laying from three to six finely spotted cream coloured eggs. Feeds on aquatic plants, seeds, insects, snails and small fish. Their presence is often noticed by the growling 'churr' sound they emit from among the reeds. In Afrikaans: Swart Riethaan.

79. Redchested Flufftail *Sarothrura rufa* 16 cm R205

Field Identification: The adult male has the whole head, neck, upper chest and upper back a deep reddish chestnut. All the remaining plumage is black lightly streaked with white. Eyes dark brown, bill dusky brown, legs dark greyish brown. The female is brown on head and neck, pale beige below, with the other plumage blackish barred and spotted with buff. Young birds are black with white flecks.

Distribution: Inhabits thick, rank growth in marshes, and is seen swimming with tail erect. Probably resident in swamps and has been known to breed at Klawervlei in the month of November.

Notes: Flies very little and then for only short distances. Lives on ants, snails and seeds found in the undergrowth. The call is a continuous 'duehh, duehh, duehh' re-

peated for about fifteen seconds, also a call like 'haw-bo', and various humming and rapid squeaky cheeping notes. One is more apt to hear the Redchested Flufftail call after sunset or on dull overcast days. Breeding in the Cape takes place from November to January when from three to five white eggs are laid in a nest constructed from grass fronds, lined with rootlets, or made of dead leaves. It will be found tucked away in reeds at ground level. In Afrikaans: Rooibors-vleikuiken.

80. Purple Gallinule *Porphyrio porphyrio* 46 cm R208

Field Identification: As can be seen from the photograph this is a large colourful bird with heavy red legs and almost comically large red feet. The crown, back of neck, sides, lower chest, belly and underparts are a bright bluish purple, with sides of face,

throat and chest iridiscent greenish turquoise. The back is green and under tail-coverts are white. The red bill and frontal shield are very conspicuous. Eyes red. The female is the same and young birds are a dull brownish colour with reddish brown legs.

Distribution: Resident in the south western Cape and breeds on vleis near Cape Town though the numbers become very much depleted during the winter months. Widely distributed throughout the area and particularly common at Verloren Vlei.

Notes: Flies heavily with slow wingbeat and trailing legs. Commonly seen walking about in shallow waters where there are thick reed beds. Has a curious high-stepping gait. Breeding time is from September to January. The nest, made of reeds, is placed well above water levels and four to five pinkish buff eggs with brownish and slate markings are laid. Feeds on insects, plants, roots and sometimes eats the eggs of other nesting birds. Has a variety of calls that sound like a variety of grunts, shrieks or even groans. In Afrikaans: Koningriethaan.

81. Moorhen *Gallinula chloropus* 34 cm R210

Field Identification: General greyish black plumage with a red shield and yellow-tipped red bill. The mantle and wings show a wash of olivy brown and there are a few white streaks on the flanks. The fairly short tail is black with under tail-coverts both black and white. Legs are olivy yellow with a red band above the tarsal joint below

the plumage, eyes red. The female has similar colouring and young birds are paler with buff streaks on flanks and with shield and bill a greenish grey.

Distribution: Resident on permanent vleis, dams and marshes where there is adequate vegetation for cover in the form of rushes and reeds.

Notes: Flies quite well with conspicuous dangling legs. When frightened will run for cover with head held low down. Swims, wades in vleis and dams, as seen in the photograph, and at times ventures into adjoining grasslands. Feeds on soft vegetable matter and seeds, and insects picked from the surface of the water. Breeds from August to December though one breeding in June has been recorded. The nest is a neat construction of rushes and reeds found in the shelter of thick vegetation or occasionally in the lower branches of a tree standing in water. Eggs number four to six and are dark beige with brown and slate blotches. The call is a cheerful descending 'kr-rrrk'. In Afrikaans: Waterhoender, in Sotho: Khokhonoka.

82. Redknobbed Coot *Fulica cristata* 43 cm R212

Field Identification: A large plump bird with dark grey plumage all over except the head and neck which are black. The frontal shield and bill form a strong contrast in snow white. The red knob above the shield is not very conspicuous out of the breeding season during which time it enlarges considerably as can be seen in the photo-

graph. The eyes are red, legs greenish grey. Females are the same and immature birds are much lighter – almost an ashy brown with a few white edges to some of the plumage.

Distribution: Resident on swamps and vleis throughout the south western Cape. Some Redknobbed Coots travel long distances and birds ringed in the Western Transvaal have been recovered at Rondevlei, while others ringed at Rondevlei have been found at George and at Mooi River in Natal.

Notes: Seen commonly and, when not in the breeding season, in large flocks. When breeding, from October to November, they are inclined to become very pugnacious and fighting is a regular occurence if other birds come near the nest. Will chase each other, almost running along the surface of the water. When in flight the feet extend beyond the tail. Feed on water plants and insects. The nest is large and cup-shaped, formed from trailing water plants. Eggs number three or more, round shaped in a stone colour with a few purplish-brown markings. The call is a humming 'v-v-v-v-v', a snorting 'tcholf', and a nasal toned 'coot'. In Afrikaans: Bleshoender, in Sotho: Mokhetle, in Xhosa: Unompemvana.

83. Blue Crane *Anthropoides paradisea* 106 cm R216

Field Identification: A graceful slender bird with flowing plumage sweeping to the ground and rather a large head on a long slim neck. The top and back of the head are a very light greyish white. The rest of the plumage is light bluish grey except that the upper portion of the neck is darker and the long secondaries, which curve right down to the ground, are black. The long legs are black, the bill pinkish yellow, eyes dark brown. Females are similar but slightly smaller and immature birds lack the full plumage and have very light chestnut colouring on the top of the head.

Distribution: Found generally near water and more rarely in drier areas usually in pairs, but possibly when migrating, in large flocks. Were originally found mainly in the Karoo and grassveld areas but are now recorded fairly commonly in the south western Cape.

Notes: The national bird of South Africa. Ornamental birds sometimes bought to grace the lawn of a lovely home but fairly dangerous due to their habit of pecking at the eyes or the ankles of unwary children. Will feed on grain, fish, small animals and reptiles. Eggs are laid on the bare ground or in a 'suggestion' of a nest formed from small stones. They have an elongated shape and are brownish yellow in colour with blotches of brown and olive green. The sound these birds make is a loud rattling croak. The male makes a low-pitched 'krurrrk' and the female an often repeated higher-pitched 'krrrrrk'. In Afrikaans: Bloukraan, in Zulu: u-Mcinsi, in Xhosa: i-Quqolo, and in Sotho: Mothlathomo.

84. Stanley Bustard *Neotis denhami* 100 – 107 cm male; 80 – 87 cm female R219

Field Identification: The adult male has crown black with a broken white central stripe, sides of face, front neck and upper chest light grey with full plumage on the upper chest. Sides of neck white and hind neck chestnut. Back brown finely vermiculated with black and whitish. Upper wing coverts black streaked with white, tail black banded with white, underparts white. Female has front neck and chest patterned in black and buff, centre of crown white and less black and white on wings. Immature birds resemble the female. Eyes are light brown, bill horn with a dark tip, legs yellowish.

Distribution: Most numerous in years of drought. Reported regularly from the bredasdorp and Swellendam districts as well as from Veloren Vlei, Stellenbosch and Velddrift. Recorded breeding in Bredasdorp. Found in grassy country with or without trees.

Notes: Usually found in pairs or small parties but difficult to approach or photograph as they are an extremely wary species and will walk away then take to flight and disappear. In the breeding season the males display by inflating their neck pouches and

dancing. Said to live on almost anything so great is the variety of food which they eat – various insects, a variety of vegetable matter and small animals. The call sounds almost like a bark and when displaying to the female the sound emitted by the male is loud and booming. Breeding takes place from October to December. No nest is constructed but a slight scrape in the earth will be used to hold two pale olivy-brown eggs smudged with darker brown and grey. Incubation is by both sexes. In Afrikaans: Veldpou.

85. Black Korhaan *Eupodotis afra* 53 cm R225

Field Identification: White ear-coverts on a black background colouring face and neck are distinctive, crown mottled and remaining underparts black. Upper parts are finely barred with black and white and a white band runs across the nape of the neck and down the sides of the chest. Bill is greyish with a pink base, eyes light brown, legs a bright yellow. The female has the head and neck as well as the back and tail pale rufous finely barred with black, the chest is white and underparts and under tail-coverts black. Immature birds resemble the female but have longitudinal stripes on the head.

Distribution: Found in a variety of habitats from coastal sand-dunes to indigenous bush and most frequent in coastal Renoster-bosveld.

Notes: Males are noisy and conspicuous, females shy and quiet, difficult to flush from protective covering. Food is derived from seeds, insects and a variety of vegetable matter. Breeding takes place from August to October and at this time the male displays by slowly dropping down uttering loud 'krracker, kkracker' sounds accompanied by fast flapping wingbeats. The nest is a grass lined scrape in the ground extremely difficult to find due to the secretive ways of the female. One or two olive green eggs are laid. In Afrikaans: Swart Korhaan.

86. African Jaçana *Actophilornis africanus* 30 cm R228

Field Identification: An attractive brightly coloured reddish chestnut bird with the top of the head and the back of neck glossy black, throat and front of neck white, and upper chest bright gold. The long grey bill is sharply pointed below the slate blue frontal shield, eyes dark brown, legs and very large feet grey. The female is similar and immature birds have upper parts tinged with green, the frontal shield is scarcely noticeable, and they are white below.

Distribution: There was an influx in the early 1970's which failed, however, to really establish itself, although the African Jaçana has been recorded as breeding in the area. Previously considered a rare vagrant. Found singly or in pairs feeding around the perimeter of weed infested stagnant dams or lakes. Still fairly rare in the south western Cape.

Notes: Nicknamed the Lily-trotter due to its habit of running over aquatic vegetation, especially water-lilies. When in flight the legs and toes are extended and this species will dive and swim in search of food. Lives on aquatic larvae, insects, snails and seeds. Often distinguished by the characteristic way it has of raising its wings after landing. Has both a coot-like call and a rattling screetch uttered in flight. Breeding takes place in the summer months from November to March and the highly polished tan-yellow eggs, covered with scroll-like marks in black, are laid in a floating nest formed from aquatic plants. Sometimes the nest is moved if it threatens to be flooded. Young chicks are sometimes seen being carried about under the wings of the adult bird. In Afrikaans: Langtoon, in Zulu: Matenda-lazebu.

87. Painted Snipe *Rostratula benghalensis* 26 cm R230

Field Identification: The male is not as brightly coloured as the female, having a dull olivy brown colouring on hind neck, back and chest, which at a distance appears almost greyish and specked. There is a distinct white marking around the eye and a golden streak over the crown, as well as two conspicuous golden bars over the shoulder and down the length of the back. Golden markings on the wings are conspicuous in flight. The back is barred with black and white, and the throat is light, the upper chest and neck black speckled with white, chest, belly and underparts white. Eyes dark brown, long bill purplish brown, legs and feet vary from a dull greyish blue to a dull yellowish green. The female has neck and upper chest a rich chestnut colour banded below with a broad white band, upper parts are olivy black, eyestrip and underparts white. Young birds resemble the male.

Distribution: A secretive bird resident in swamps and marshes and present throughout the south western Cape, though difficult to spot as they hide in the reeds bordering stretches of water.

Notes: Painted snipe are slow in flight and their rounded wings and dangling legs become identifiable features. When alarmed they will freeze in one position and tend to merge with their surroundings in an attempt at camouflage. Breeding time in the Cape is from August to November. The male is the more active partner in preparing the nest, which is a shallow depression, lined with thin broken reeds. The eggs number from three to five, yellow in colour with many black markings. This species feeds on insect larvae, grass seed and worms, and has a croaking guttural call, that of the male being the more shrill. In Afrikaans: Goudsnip.

88. Black Oystercatcher *Haematopus moquini* 51 cm R231

Field Identification: Very easy to identify as this Oystercatcher is entirely black with bright red eyes surrounded by orange, an orange-tipped red bill and red legs. Females are the same and young birds are a duller mottled brown-black with underparts whitish and legs brownish orange.

Distribution: Widely distributed along the Cape coast, yet very sparingly in places. To be seen on rocky coasts and beaches and at lagoons and estuaries.

Notes: Found sometimes in flocks of up to forty consisting mainly of young birds feeding along the water level, probing the wet sand to the full length of their long bills, and prising mussels from rocky crevices. Feed on molluscs, crustacea and annelids. Breeding time is from October to March. One to four eggs are laid in a slight

hollow lined with bits of debris or a few pieces of broken shells, The eggs are stone-coloured, with blotches varying from pale purple to dark blackish brown as can be seen in the photograph. The alarm call is a series of sharp 'pip pip pip' sounds and another call is a clear repeated 'klee-weep'. In Afrikaans: Tobie.

89. Turnstone *Arenaria interpres* 23 cm R232

Field Identification: In winter plumage the head is grey and white, the upper parts brown mottled with grey and white. The throat and underparts are white with a broad mottled grey and white band across the chest. The eyes are dark brown, the pointed bill black and the legs orange. Many Turnstone, like the one photographed here, have changed to partial breeding plumage before migrating overseas as the winter months approach – at that time the upper parts become a bright chestnut and the head and underparts are more distinctly black and white.

Distribution: A summer migrant from the Palaearctic found along the coast and on offshore islands. Common at Langebaan. To be found during spring and summer until April but some birds do remain during the winter.

Notes: The Turnstone does not breed at the Cape but this species is to be seen usually in small flocks of up to twenty – although occasionally in large flocks where food is plentiful. Feed on small crustacea and molluscs found between exposed rocks at low tide. When disturbed they fly away low over the water uttering their call of 'kit-it-it-it' or 'chidda-chidda-chidda'. Courtship is often seen before the Turnstone departs on its migration to the breeding grounds. In Afrikaans: Steenloper.

90. Ringed Plover *Charadrius hiaticula* 16 cm R233

Field Identification: The orange yellow legs form a distinct identification at all stages of the Ringed Plover's development. The forehead, throat and neck are white as are the lower chest and underparts. The crown, back and wings are an ashy chestnut brown. There is a dark blackish brown band around the neck which extends downwards on either side of the chest, a second similar band from the base of the bill under the eye and along the side of the face, and a third on the crown between the eyes and above the white forehead strip. Inner primaries have white patches which are seen as a white bar in flight. The eyes are brown, bill orangy brown with a darker tip. The female is similar and young birds are duller above, have no black band on the head, and the chest band is usually incomplete and not as dark as in the adult bird.

Distribution: To be found at tidal mudflats and vleis, including irrigation lakes and large farm dams. A common non-breeding summer migrant from the Palaearctic. First arrivals reach Cape Town by late September but most do not arrive until the beginning of December, leaving again in March or April or occasionally staying until early May, or even remaining for the entire winter. Birds ringed at Rondevlei are on record as returning from the U.S.S.R. and France.

Notes: The legs of the Ringed Plover move so rapidly when running that they re almost invisible. Usually fly low and resettle at a short distance and then run off once more. Seen in small parties along the edges of water where they run rapidly stopping suddenly to pick up food and then run on with the head held up at all times except when actually pecking. Feed on insects, crustacea and molluscs, and continue feeding day and night depending on the tides. The call is a melodic 'too-ti' or 'tiuu-it'. In Afrikaans: Ringnek-strandlopertjie, in Xhosa: Unokrekre.

91. Whitefronted Sandplover *Charadrius marginatus* 9 cm R235

Field Identification: The female is seen in the accompanying photograph, the male having a darker band across the forehead and through the eye, as well as usually having darkish patches on each side of the chest. In both sexes the forehead, hind collar, sides of face and underparts are white, the chest being lightly washed with palest beige. Eyes brown, bill and legs black, crown and upper parts light ashy brown mix with pale chestnut, flight feathers pale greyish brown, central tail feathers black. The feet do not extend beyond the tail feathers in flight. Young birds lack the forehead band, underparts are white, nestlings are greyish above with black markings.

Distribution: Found on sandy beaches and dunes along the coastline, as well as in sandy areas near rivers and inland lakes.

Notes: The action of its legs in running is so rapid that they become almost invisible and the bird appears to glide over the sand. Usually seen singly or in pairs. Have a characteristic sideways movement and will rise from the ground with a soft 'twit', flying very low to a nearby point and then continue running rapidly. The head is always upright except for the moment it takes to peck an insect from the sand. Lives on crustacea, insect larvae and worms. As will be seen in the photograph the nest is a shallow scrape in the sand and a few of these scrape are usually constructed before the female eventually lays her eggs, which as can be seen, are buff with brown markings, kept half buried in the sand. This method aids a small bird to keep the rather large eggs warm. In Afrikaans: Vaal Strandlopertjie.

92. Chestnutbanded Sandplover *Caharadrius pallidus*
15 cm R236

Field Identification: The male is pale grey above with wing feathers lightly brushed with a tawny chestnut and the tail feathers tipped with black. There is a black forehead band edged with chestnut as well as a black band from the bill and through the eye. The forehead, chin and sides of face are white, as are the underparts and chest, the latter having a chestnut band, except in the first plumage. Eyes dark brown, bill black, legs olivy grey. The female lacks the black band and from a distance is sometimes mistaken for the Whitefronted Sandplover except that this species appears plumper. Young birds have no black on the head.

Distribution: Found at saltpans with movements controlled by rising and falling water levels. Common on the Berg River and at the south end of the Langebaan Lagoon as well as at Ysterfontein, where this picture was taken, and at Bredasdorp.

Notes: Usually found singly or in pairs – a much shyer bird than the Whitefronted Sandplover. Flies off low over the ground when in the least disturbed. Breeds during April and from September to December. The nest is to be found in open sandy areas or on stony ground, being a shallow scrape sometimes lined with bits of shells. Eggs number two and are putty coloured with sepia and grey markings. In flight a soft 'twirit' is uttered and when alarmed a loud 'kittup' or a drawn out 'churr'. In Afrikaans: Rooiband-strandlopertjie.

93. Kittlitz's Sandplover *Charadrius pecuarius* 16 cm R237

Field Identification: A distinguishing mark of this species is the black band over the forehead curving downwards behind the eye and meeting behind the nape of the neck, forming a border to the white-edged brownish crown and nape. In the female this line is dark brown instead of black. Wing feathers a tawny brown, throat, chest and underparts white, washed with a very pale golden tawny. Eyes are brown, pointed bill black, legs greyish black. In flight the feet extend beyond the tail feathers. Young birds have no black or white on the head, being tinted buff with darker markings brown.

Distribution: Common in the south western Cape beside vleis and lagoons, on open commons and aerodromes, even occupying open ground in the city of Cape Town between the buildings and the seafront. Usually seen in small flocks but occasionally numbering as many as one hundred or more. Found also on offshore islands.

Notes: These plovers are not very shy and if disturbed will fly for a short distance quickly settling down again. When with young they will put on an 'injured act' to draw attention away from the chicks. Food is derived from insects, larvae and crustacea. The call is similar to that of the Whitefronted Sandplover, 'trit-trittrittrit' also an alarm call 'prrt' and a 'tip-peep' when in flight. Breed mainly from July to November, laying two creamy coloured eggs fairly thickly covered with black overlapping lines. The nest is a scrape in a stretch of flat land filled with twigs, dried grass or dung. These materials are used to cover the eggs when the adult leaves the nest. In Afrikaans: Geelbors-strandlopertjie.

94. Threebanded Sandplover *Charadrius tricollaris* 18 cm R238

Field Identification: Immediately identifiable by the two black bands across the chest separated by a white one, as well as a white band encircling the brown crown. There is a conspicuous white wing bar and a white terminal band to the tail feathers.

Underparts white, upper parts dull brown, bill black-tipped with a pinky red base, legs flesh coloured, brown eyes surrounded by a red wattle. Females are the same and young birds have an incomplete brown upper chest band and are more generally buff and brown.

Distribution: Often seen in pairs on muddy shores at the water's edge of lagoons, rivers, vleis and dams throughout the south western Cape. Sometimes found on the seashore.

Notes: Flies with a distinctive jerky flight and is often discovered first by its high-pitched noisy 'wick-wick' or 'tiuu-it, tiuu-it' and subsequently seen standing still, with its body slanting forward, bobbing up and down with each call. On alighting their tails move up and down, and, like many other plovers, they are inclined to run in starts. Sometimes occur in flocks of up to thirty or forty birds but more usually singly or in small family parties. Live on insects taken on land or from the water, crustacea, small molluscs and worms. Breeding time in the Cape is from August to November and two large creamy eggs, covered in brownish lines, forming two darker rings, are laid. These are clearly seen in the photograph. The nest is a small depression in the ground edged with shells or pebbles. In Afrikaans: Drieband-strandlopertjie, in Xhosa: Unokrekre.

95. Grey Plover *Pluvialis squatarola* 30 cm R241

Field Identification: In winter plumage the general impression is of a medium-sized bird speckled dark grey and white above, with underparts white, tail feathers black. In flight the black feathers under the wings (likened to dirty armpits) are a conspicuous aid to identification. As summer approaches black marks appear on the chest and belly, until the whole area from chin to the lower belly is totally black with a white margin. The upper markings become darker and the white stands out in greater contrast. Eyes are dark brown and the long legs grey.

Distribution: Occur along the entire south western Cape coastline. The Grey Plover does not breed in the south western Cape however, being a summer migrant from

the Palaearctic to salt water marshes, tidal mud-flats and lagoons. Seen regularly at saltpans and on rocky stretches of coastline until early April. Further up the warmer western coast they will remain through the winter.

Notes: Occur in large flocks and have the usual upright stance and typical habit of running in starts common to all Plovers. Prior to their departure towards the end of March they will put on more fat and appear plumper, as well as beginning to assume breeding plumage. Feed on crustacea and small molluscs found in the tidal mudflats. Their call is a pleasant far-carrying 'tlui-tlui'. In Afrikaans: Grys Strandloper.

96. Crowned Plover *Vanellus coronatus* 30 cm R242

Field Identification: A distinctive black crown almost like a hood, stretching from the top of the bill, over the forehead and down to the nape, encircled by a white band, distinguishes this plover from any other species. The chest is a darkish sand, separated from the white belly by a black band. Flight feathers are dark sand above with under-wing coverts, under-tail coverts, rump and tail white, the latter having a broad black terminal band. Females are similar and young birds have circlet of paler tipped down, and sandy chest plumage merging into an ash brown breast band. The bill and legs are orange-red in adults, eyes yellow-orange. Young birds have eyes biscuit or more rarely brown, bill and legs greenish yellow.

Distribution: A very common resident species found throughout the south west Cape. Shows a preference for open country where the grass is short.

Notes: Found after the breeding season in fairly large flocks but at other times usually in pairs or very small parties. An extremely upright stance is noticeable when standing still and when feeding the insect is pecked with a forward thrust of the head. Food is derived from grasshoppers, beetles, caterpillars and ladybirds. Breeding takes place at any time throughout the year but especially from August to December, the nest being a scrape on gravelly or cultivated land. Occasionally the nest is lined with stones or twigs. About three eggs are laid of an olive brown colour. In Afrikaans: Kiewietjie, in Xhosa: Igxiya, in Zulu: Mbagaqwa.

97. Blackwinged Plover *Vanellus melanopterus* 27 cm R243

Field Identification: Head, neck, nape and chest greyish brown with a white mark on the forehead and extending over the eye. Upper parts bronzy brown, tail white with a subterminal black band, secondaries white with black tips. A broad black band separates the neck and chest colouring from the white belly and underparts. Eyes yellow with a red rim, bill black, legs greyish red. The female is similar and young birds have no dark band on the chest.

Distribution: Rare in the south western Cape but recently increasing (particularly in the Overberg). Has been seen recently in the Somerset West district. Found in open bush country particularly on land grazed by large herds of game or stock paddocks. Has a preference for moister localities.

Notes: A migrant although some remain in their wintering areas all the year round. Found most often in small flocks but during the winter are more social and will congregate in flocks of up to fifty birds. Feed on beetles and insect larvae found in droppings, as well as grubs, worms and flies. In flight and when alighting with wings raised, the white under wing-coverts become a distinguishing feature. The call varies in pitch and intensity sometimes rising to a high-pitched screamed 'che-che-che-chereck'. More usually 'titihoya' is the call uttered in flight. Breeding takes place from August to October. Eggs number three or four, a dark olivy brown with numerous black smudgy marks. The eggs are found in a hollow scraped in the soil, often on a rise, and usually with the thinner end buried so that only the wider end is to be seen. In Afrikaans: Swartvlerk-kiewietjie, in Zulu: i-Titihoya.

98. Blacksmith Plover *Vanellus armatus* 30 cm R245

Field Identification: The general impression is a patchy black and white with upper wing-coverts and scapulars grey. The forehead, crown, back of neck and upper tail-coverts are white, with back of head, sides of face, throat, chest and breast black. The tail, with its broad black terminal band, and underparts, are white. The pointed bill is black, legs blackish grey and eyes dark red. Females are similar and nestlings are mottled sandy and black above with underparts white.

Distribution: Very common and abundant on vleis since its relatively recent establishment in the south western Cape. Favours damp situations and a typical area to find this species would be where flood or dam waters spill over onto flat grasslands.

Notes: The name is derived from the fact that the Blacksmith Plover sounds like a busy little blacksmith beating a hammer on an anvil the call being a clear 'tink-tink-tink'. Found in pairs or very small groups and distinguished in flight by a slow rhythmic wingbeat. Unlike the Crowned Plover it is a quiet bird unless disturbed. Feeds on insects and worms. Breeds from July to November in the Cape, the nest being a shallow depression in the soil, near water, lined with twigs, grass and even pebbles. Eggs number three or four and have a light olivy grey background with many dark grey mudges, clearly seen in the photograph. In Afrikaans: Bontkiewietjie.

99. Ethiopian Snipe *Gallinago nigripennis* 28 cm R250

Field Identification: Generally a mottled black, brown and buff above, and white below, with longitudinal streaks down the crown, and a buff eye stripe. The neck, chest and sides are also mottled and streaked. Legs greenish brown or greenish yellow, eyes brown, very long pointed bill black towards the tip and brown and black towards the base. In flight the wings appear rounded and the outer tail feathers are barred. The female and young birds are similar.

Distribution: Resident, breeding mid-winter, and to be found on swamps and marshes. When the water dries up they will move to another habitat.
Notes: Found singly or in pairs and feed on larvae or insects, worms and crustacea. The grass-woven nest is hidden beneath a tuft of grass, the blades of which are pulled over and secured both to hide it and to give protection from the sun. Two glossy, pointed, olivy-buff eggs, with a variety of blotches of colour, are laid. Ethiopian Snipe put on aerial displays during the breeding season and until the eggs are hatched, and make a drumming noise by vibrating the two outer tail feathers against each other in flight. The sound they utter is a quiet 'tchek'. In Afrikaans: Afrikaanse Snip, in Xhosa: Umnqunduluti, in Zulu: u-Nununde, and in Sotho: Koekoelemao.

100. Curlew Sandpiper *Calidris ferruginea* 25 cm R251

Field Identification: A medium sized wader which when non-breeding appears in greyish brown plumage above, dark tail feathers and white underparts. In silhouette there is a hunched curve to the back which curves down to the rump. There is a light eye patch and the under tail-coverts are white, showing a white patch at the base of the tail in flight and a white wing bar. The upper chest is washed with pale grey. Eyes are dark brown and the long rather heavy bill, pointed downwards at the tip, is olive-tinted black, legs olivy brown. Females are similar and young birds resemble adult birds in non-breeding plumage. During the breeding season the upper parts

are mottled black and chestnut, underparts a bright but lighter chestnut.

Distribution: Prolific non-breeding summer migrants from the Palaearctic found near fresh water and at the coast. First-year birds remain for the Cape winter in considerable numbers. Most arrive, chiefly from Russia, towards the end of November and leave by the beginning of March, though the period between arrival and departure may be considerably extended.

Notes: Active, lively and highly gregarious, found in large flocks particularly on open mud-flats. Typically their bodies are held horizontally as they walk about probing their bills to the full extent in their search for food, which is made up of worms and crustacea, the head being lifted up between probes. Rest closely huddled in flocks and are liable to stretch their wings upwards before moving away if disturbed. Will fly in flocks uttering a whistled 'chirrip', and pairs chasing each other make a 'chit-chit' sound. Interesting migration records are from Paarden Island to Russia, covering a distance of over 14,000 kms, and from Rondevlei to Russia, a distance of 10,600 kms. There have also been recoveries of ringed birds in Angola, Zaire and Iran. In Afrikaans: Krombek-strandloper.

101. Little Stint *Calidris minuta* 14 cm R253

Field Identification: The Little Stint is smaller in size and with a shorter bill than the Curlew Sandpiper, with which it is often confused. As the name would suggest this is the smallest of the waders, as well as being the smallest of the migrants. It seems amazing that such a small bird will fly from the Cape to Russia and Iran. The non-breeding plumage is a drab mottled ashy grey on crown, nape and general upper parts, with upper tail-coverts, centre of rump and two central tail feathers blackish, underparts white. Above the bill there is a white patch and there is a light eye stripe. In flight two white V-shaped marks, facing different directions, become evident on the back, as well as white wing bars. Eyes and legs black. The female resembles the male. Breeding plumage is a deeper mottled black and tawny, with underparts white. Some birds are in partial breeding plumage before migrating.

Distribution: Abundant at temporary vleis and marine environments in the south western Cape from spring until late April or the early part of May, with a few birds remaining for the winter.

Notes: Most of the time is spent busily feeding with head kept down all the time, pecking from side to side as the bird moves forward. Food is derived from crustacea, mosquitoes and larvae. Inclined to fly in flocks twittering continuously. The call of the Little Stint has been described as a twittering repeated 'chit', or 'whit', or 'tit'! In Afrikaans: Klein Strandloper.

102. Knot *Calidris canutus* 25 cm R254

Field Identification: This species is sometimes confused with the Ruff but can be distinguished by more uniform colouring on upper parts and dark legs. Smaller than the Grey Plover with a longer tapering bill and a plump appearance. The chest takes on a chestnut colouring in April before departing. Eyes brown, bill black, legs dark olivy green.

Distribution: A summer migrant from the Palaearctic found in salt water areas. Common at Langebaan, where ringed birds from Britain and Belgium have been recovered, and at Berg River.

Notes: Usually occurs singly, at the coast, but flocks of up to 150 have been recorded both at Langebaan and at Walvis Bay. Single birds sometimes join flocks of other species. The photograph showing a Knot probing the sand, which it does several times before stepping forward, is typical. The flight pattern is swift and strong, the call being a single 'knut' rarely sounded. In Afrikaans: Knoet.

103. Sanderling *Calidris alba* 19 cm R255

Field Identification: A rather drab colouring, mainly white in appearance but with pale grey on crown and upper parts. Two distinctive features are a black shoulder marking and the fact that this species has no hind toe, leaving only three instead of the usual four, which is clearly seen in the photograph taken in Europe. In flight there is a distinct white wing bar bordered by pale grey, on the forward wing plumage, and darkish colouring on the back edge of the wings. The breeding plumage is not often recorded but at that time the head, back and upper chest are speckled with chestnut and the wing feathers darken. Eyes brown, bill and legs black.

Distribution: A summer migrant from the Palaearctic, common along the west coast and more rarely recorded singly inland as well. Ringed birds are recorded returning from England and Malta and a bird ringed at Langebaan was recovered in the U.S.S.R. Flocks of up to fifty birds are known to winter in the Gamtoos River area.

Notes: Plump little birds seen along sandy beaches where they feed on small creatures thrown up by the breaking waves. Their food is derived from crustacea, molluscs, larvae and remnants of small fish. They make furrows in the sand with their bills and keep their heads permanently down while feeding. Their call is a whistled 'twick twick'. In Afrikaans: Drietoon-strandloper.

104. Ruff *Philomachus pugnax* 30 cm R256

Field Identification: The male is 30 cm but the female is about 23 cm. The upper parts are lightish brown with a mottled effect caused by light edging to the plumage. The brown becomes darker on the back and wings. There is a white area above the black bill and around the brown eye, and the throat and underparts are white. The long legs vary from a dirty olivy green to orange, the latter colour causing a certain amount of confusion with the Redshank, but the legs and bill are shorter than in that species and there is no red on the bill. When in flight the Ruff shows a distinct barred brown line down the centre of the rump, with a white oval on either side, and the tail tip is light brown. Rarely do we have the opportunity to see the beautiful ruffs the males acquire during the breeding season, as by that time they have migrated to their breeding grounds in the northern hemisphere. Female is similar except when male is in breeding plumage.

Distribution: Probably the most common non-breeding summer migrant from the Palaearctic. Found at vleis, on the banks of inland waters and in short vegetation in the proximity of water. Not found on sandy beaches or at salt water marshes or lagoons. Birds ringed at the Cape have been recovered in the U.S.S.R. and have returned.

Notes: The Ruff has a distinctive erect stance when alarmed. Found in flocks of a dozen or so to about two hundred, but there have been recordings of flocks numbering about 1,000 birds. Strong fliers flying with a regular wing beat. Sometimes found in wheat fields, they feed on seeds, worms, insects, crustacea and molluscs. No sound has been recorded from these birds during their stay in this country. In Afrikaans: Kemphaan.

105. Terek Sandpiper *Xenus cinereus* 23 cm R257

Field Identification: Light greyish brown above with a long slender upturned black bill, lighter at the base. The wing shoulders are black, and when in breeding plumage, as seen in the photograph, there are black streaks on mantle and scapulars. White below and white tips to secondaries which are conspicuous in flight. There is also a light eye stripe and a pale rump, as distinguishing features. Shortish legs are orange yellow, eyes dark brown.

Distribution: A rare, non-breeding summer migrant to coastal lagoons, but a regular species at Langebaan. The only ringed return to date is from the U.S.S.R. The photograph was taken in Europe.

Notes: A very active bird having a characteristic way of bobbing its hindquarters as it busily probes the full length of its beak. Will run at great speed and is most often seen perched on partially submerged trees, where it will roost for the night. Lives on aquatic insects, molluscs and crustacea. The call is a clear whistling 'tu-tu-tu', uttered either in flight or when perched. In Afrikaans: Terekruiter.

106. Common Sandpiper *Tringa hypoleucos* 19 cm R258

Field Identification: Upper parts are an olivy grey with a slight golden sheen. The neck and upper chest are paler and lightly streaked with white, underparts white. The bill is dark grey, the eyes brown and there is a light eyebrow, and a white patch on the shoulder. A white bar on the wings is conspicuous in flight. Legs are greyish. Females resemble the male and young birds have upper parts mottled. During the breeding season the upper parts have dark streaks and bars, which may be seen prior to their leaving for the north in early May.

Distribution: Not very prolific in the south western Cape. A non-breeding summer migrant found near fresh water, on rocky coasts and on offshore islands.

Notes: Characteristic flight is skimming over a stretch of water with spasmodic wing action alternately flying and then gliding. When feeding both the head and the hind part of the body will bob. The bill is probed only half way into the mud to find larvae, molluscs and crustacea. The Common Sandpiper has a high twittering call or a high-pitched 'tsee-see-see', and is usually found alone or in pairs. In Afrikaans: Gewone Ruiter.

107. Marsh Sandpiper *Tringa stagnitilis* 23 cm R262

Field Identification: Upper parts ashy grey, lower back and rump white. Could be described as a smaller version of the Greenshank with wing feathers a little lighter.

The thin black tapering bill and lack of any wing bar distinguish it from the Redshank. Legs vary in colour from orange yellow to dull olive green, and are long and thin. Females are similar and young birds have the crown and nape marked with dark blotches, with the plumage on the upper parts edged with white. In breeding plumage the Marsh Sandpiper is darkly mottled on upper parts.

Distribution: A common non-breeding summer migrant from the Palaearctic to vleis, marshes, lagoons and occasionally to the coast. Sometimes remains for the winter but most arrive towards the end of the year and leave before March.

Notes: Lively little birds often seen in the company of the larger Greenshanks and with other waders, either singly or in small flocks, or even in flocks of up to one hundred birds. When in flight the long legs and toes extend far beyond the tail feathers. Feed on small molluscs, crustacea and insect larvae. An alarm call is a single 'tchick' which when uttered by a flock resembles a flock of Wood Sandpipers. More usually one hears a clear 'tee-oo'. In Afrikaans: Moerasruiter.

108. Greenshank *Tringa nebularia* 32 cm   R263

Field Identification: Upper parts are greyish with plumage edged in white giving a mottled effect. The head and neck are very light, streaked with grey, the lower back and rump white. The shoulder and under wing-coverts are blackish, the tail light brown down the centre, otherwise white barred with brown. The long, slightly upturned bill is bluish grey from the base with the lower half black, legs greenish grey, eyes brown. The female is the same and young birds have upper plumage edged with buff and chest dotted with brown. When breeding upper parts darken to a mottled blackish colour and the flanks are marked with brown.

Distribution: Another common non-breeding summer migrant from the Palaearctic visiting vleis, marshes, lagoons, pools or the open coast, and staying during winter fairly often.

Notes: Flies off with much gusto if disturbed shrieking a loud triple call. Always found near water whether the open coast or small roadside pools. Feeds on insects, molluscs and crustacea. Usually arrives in August and leaves by the end of April and during that period is seen singly, in small parties, or in flocks of up to 150 birds. Wades around in water which may be as deep as its legs are long, picking insects off the surface or probing its bill into the sand. The call is a clear carrying 'tew-tew-tew'. In Afrikaans: Groenpoot-ruiter.

109. Wood Sandpiper *Tringa glareola* 20 cm R264

Field Identification: The head is white with brown and blackish streaks extending down throat and chest, upper parts mottled brown and white, tail white barred with brownish, underparts white. Eyes dark brown, long bill black at tip and dark greenish olive at base, legs olive to orange yellow. Females are similar, young spotted with gold. During the breeding season the plumage becomes darker and streaked with brown.

Distribution: A common migrant arriving in the early spring towards the end of August and leaving in autumn, during the early part of May, with some birds remaining for the winter. Seen at tidal mudflats and lagoons as well as temporary vleis and flooded fields.

Notes: One is more likely to see single birds, but flocks of up to fifty of this species have been recorded. Typically they are found paddling around the edges of waterlogged fields pecking off the surface. Live on insects, frogs, small crustacea, spiders or small fish. Characteristically stretch their necks and bob up and down before flying off into nearby vegetation when disturbed, with a shrill 'chiff-iff-iff'. In Afrikaans: Bosruiter.

110. Bar-tailed Godwit *Limosa lapponica* 38 cm R266

Field Identification: Head, neck and chest offwhite with dusky chestnut streaks, darkest on forehead and upper back. Mantle and back chestnut and dusky, with plumage edged with offwhite. In flight the dark outer edges of the wings and the barring on the fan-shaped tail are clearly evident, the feet extending beyond the tail.

The summer plumage is a rich chestnut on head, neck and underparts. Bill flesh pink with darker brown tip, eyes brown, legs dark greenish grey.

Distribution: Very rare in the south but regular at Langebaan. A non-breeding summer migrant. Leaves early May with very few wintering. A bird ringed at Swartkops in the Eastern Province was recovered in Iran. The photograph was taken in Europe.

Notes: The flight pattern is very similar to the Whimbrel but the bill is much longer. When feeding, mostly in shallow water, the head is kept down and the long bill is probed up to its full length in the mud, in fact it is not unusual to see the head under water as well. In Afrikaans: Rosse Grutto.

111. Curlew *Numenius arquata* 59 cm R267

Field Identification: The picture, taken in Europe, shows the Curlew on the nest in breeding plumage, which is somewhat darker and more heavily streaked than when in the non-breeding season in South Africa, with the background colour pale cinnamon. The sexes are the same but males are smaller than females. Upper parts mottled black and light chestnut; neck, chest and breast buff streaked with chestnut and dusky, rump and underparts white. Eyes brown, bill greyish horn extremely long and downward curved, usually lighter at the base, legs greenish grey. Young birds are heavily mottled above.

Distribution: A non-breeding summer migrant from the Palaearctic to our coasts and to the larger vleis, over-wintering fairly regularly.

Notes: A help for easy identification is that the bill is said to be half as long as the body, appearing straight for half its length and then curving downwards. Seen most often in small parties or flocks of from fifty to sixty birds. Found on the sea coast and at estuaries as well as next to inland waters. Lives on worms and small aquatic animals such as crabs and mud prawns and probes the extremely long bill into the mud up to its full length, raising its head between feedings. The call is a resonant 'cur-lee' repeated, and a harsh 'crooee-crooee'. Has a fairly slow wingbeat but their flight is

fast and strong. The eggs, shown in a grassy hollow in the picture, are deep ivory with scattered dark markings. In Afrikaans: Wulp.

112. Whimbrel *Numenius phaeopus* 43 cm R268

Field Identification: The head, neck, chest and upper parts are mottled to a varying degree in blackish brown on a buff background leaving a distinctive light stripe over the centre crown bordered by two heavy dark stripes, seen clearly in the illustration. Like the Curlew, which it much resembles, the male is smaller than the female, but the bill is shorter than in that species. There is a lighter eyestripe, no wing bar, underparts white, but in breeding plumage the streaks continue low down over the belly. Eyes brownish, legs grey or blackish.

Distribution: More common than the Curlew preferring the sea coast. Some stay during the winter and in June of 1965 fifty six Whimbrels were counted at Langebaan Lagoon.

Notes: A rather shy bird usually seen alone or in very small flocks. Single birds may mix freely with Curlews but they tend to remain separate if in a flock. They lift their heads when feeding and the call is a long seven-syllabled 'tetti-tetti-tetti-tet' or 'peep-eep-peep-eep-peep-eep-ee' not the shorter two-syllabled call of the Curlew. In Afrikaans: Klein Wulp.

113. Blackcrowned Avocet *Recurvirostra avosetta* 43 cm R269

Field Identification: The magnificent photograph shows clearly the adult bird, the eggs and the tiny newly-hatched nestlings, on the nest sited close to water. Adults of both sexes are the same, long-legged black and white birds with a long thin, black, upturned bill and red eyes. Most of the plumage is white, with a black stripe over the head, including the eye section, and over the crown, from the bill to the nape. There is black on the wing shoulders, primaries, and in a bar across the wings. The legs are a pale greyish blue and the toes are webbed. Young birds become a buffish brown before gaining their adult plumage.

Distribution: Fairly rare, some being migrants, others resident at vleis, but inclined to move to a new locality after a period of time.

Notes: In summer the number of Avocets swells enormously with large flocks arriving from northern countries. Inclined to fly in close formation alighting on stretches of water where they wade in the shallows, moving their upturned bills from side to side in the search for aquatic insects, annelids, crustacea and molluscs. In deeper water they will 'up-end' like ducks and swim under water. From August to October three to five eggs will be found in a shallow scrape, lined with bits of twigs and grass, on a bank near water. The eggs are greenish grey in colour with lines and spots of slate and black as seen in the photograph. Two calls are recorded, a loud 'cwit-cwit-cwit' of alarm and a clear 'kleeoot' when in flight. In Afrikaans: Bont Elsie.

114. Blackwinged Stilt *Himantopus himantopus* 38 cm R270

Field Identification: The name is a perfect description of the bird with its red stilt-like legs and black wings shot through with a lustrous green sheen, in sharp contrast to the snow white of the rest of its body. Eyes are crimson, bill long, thin and black.

Mantle and scapulars of the adult female are brown instead of black, and young birds are similar, with much of the face and neck a greyish brown as well, legs pink.

Distribution: Usually seen singly but flocks do occur on permanent and temporary vleis numbering up to five hundred birds.

Notes: Typically one sees the Blackwinged Stilt paddling knee-deep in shallow water picking its food off the surface in the form of small crustacea, molluscs, and the larvae of insects. When in flight the long thin red legs extend well beyond the tail feathers. This species is reluctant to swim, is fairly tame and is not usually noisy, but if disturbed and alarmed will fly persistently over the intruder uttering a shrill alarm call like 'kik-kik-kik'. Breeding takes place from May to December, usually four stone-coloured brown-marked eggs being laid in a shallow hollow of grass and twigs on marshy ground. In Afrikaans: Rooipoot-elsie.

115. Water Dikkop *Burhinus vermiculatus* 40 cm R274

Field Identification: The head is large and rather square. Plumage has a greyish buff background with short dark streaks all over except small areas around the eye, above the beak and under the throat, as well as the underparts, which are offwhite. There is a white bar near the shoulder and the wings have a more grey toning than the plumage elsewhere. In flight a small black and white patch at the tip of the wings and a broad grey patch can be seen. Females are similar. The large pale eyes are light green, bill black with yellow at the base, legs a light yellowish green, and characterised by the absence of the hind toe.

Distribution: Less common than the Spotted Dikkop and always found near to water. Resident where there are large permanent rivers as well as bushes and trees.

Notes: Nocturnal in habits, the Water Dikkop hides under bushes during the day and if disturbed will run off with its head down or run and fly with an alternate rapid and slow wingbeat. Crustacea and insects form their diet and most of their flying and calling occurs at night, the call being a shrill clear 'whee-yu-ee' often repeated. Breeding time is from September to December. Eggs number two and vary from cream to a slightly deeper buff, marked with dark brown blotches. The eggs may be found on open ground, on sand or under bushes. In Afrikaans: Waterdikkop.

116. Spotted Dikkop *Burhinus capensis* 43 cm R275

Field Identification: Can be distinguished from the Water Dikkop by the fact that there is no white bar on the folded wing and the dark markings are more spotted or speckled than streaked. The background colour is light buff heavily marked with dull black. The very large yellow eyes are ringed with buff and black, which makes them look even larger than they are already. Underparts are buff fading to almost offwhite. The straight black bill is yellow at the base and the legs a dull yellow. In flight a small white square near the tip of the wings and a white spot on the primary coverts become conspicuous.

Distribution: Prolific throughout the open country in the south west Cape, especially the Strandveld and on offshore islands. Capetonians are familiar with the Spotted Dikkop in suburban areas like Claremont, Rondebosch and Gardens.

Notes: Very reluctant to fly when disturbed during the day and will usually run along the ground with the head held low before rising up with an unusually fast wingbeat. When resettling they will land, spread their wings and then fold them. These two photographs show the male in aggressive stance and the female with young. This species becomes especially noisy and busy on moonlit nights and their plaintive, eerie, whistling 'tchee-u' calls, often repeated and then dying away, can be quite frightening to anyone with a superstitious turn of mind! Feed on grass seed, insects, small crustacea and molluscs. Usually two eggs, cream to buff spotted

with brown, are laid during spring or early summer. Often they are found, as illustrated, on open ground or near some plant. In Afrikaans: Dikkop, in Zulu: um-Bugaqwa, in Xhosa: i-Ngqanqola, in Sotho: Tapiane.

117. Doublebanded Courser *Rhinoptilus africanus* 22 cm R278

Field Identification: Crown, mantle and upper parts have crescent-shaped tawny markings, edged with black and offwhite, of varying sizes, small on the crown and larger on the back. Sides of face, nape, neck and throat buff with blackish streaks, underparts offwhite. From the nape and round the upper chest are two widely spaced black bands. In flight the forward part of the wing is black, the rest rufous above and below, with upper tail-coverts white. The female resembles the male, eyes dark brown, bill black, legs white. Young birds have no black bands and are tawny above with plumage edged with white.

Distribution: Favours dry rocky country as seen in the photograph, often with thorn trees, and may be seen at dry pans. Recorded from a number of places in the more western areas, as far south as Malmesbury and even at Somerset West, probably only as a straggler. Fairly common in the extreme north of the area. Known to nest in September at Bossieveld, near Worcester.

Notes: This species is so well camouflaged by its cryptic colouring that often it remains invisible until it starts running. Usually occurs in pairs or small flocks scattered in sandy veld or amongst dry bushes. Reluctant to fly and runs along the ground feeding on harvester termites and ants, both by day and at night. Although it is not a noisy bird it has three different calls, one is 'woo-woo-woo-wook', another is

'chikee-chikee-chikee-kee-kee-kee' and a third is a thin reedy 'pee-wee' when put to flight. One egg is laid often amongst game droppings. It is a buff colour with lines of brown which sometimes form a band around the egg. In Afrikaans: Dubbelband-drawertjie.

118. Subantarctic Skua *Catharacta antarctica* 60 cm R286

Field Identification: A rather heavily built umber brown skua somewhat larger than other skuas. A clear identification can be made from the conspicuous white 'windows' on the primaries seen in flight and so beautifully illustrated in the accompanying photograph. The central feathers of the tail are slightly longer than the other plumage giving a slightly rounded silhouette. Certain individuals are somewhat reddish in appearance particularly around the neck. Eyes are light brown, bill and legs black.

Distribution: Present all year round and seen following ships to pick up refuse. A common non-breeding migrant from further south and sub-antarctic regions, most common in the winter.

Notes: Attacks terns or gulls with great ferocity. Usually found solitary far out at sea or off-shore, but will come right into harbours occasionally. Feeds on other birds, young of other birds, and birds eggs as well as the refuse from ships already mentioned. The call is a plaintive 'quee-kek-kek'. In Afrikaans: Bruin Roofmeeu.

119. Kelp Gull or Southern Blackbacked Gull
Larus dominicanus **60 cm R287**

Field Identification: Adult birds, both male and female, are mainly white with mantle, scapulars and wings black, the latter having a white trailing edge. Eyes are a greyish white with reddish-orange eyelids; the thick yellow bill has an orange-red tip below, and the legs and webbed feet vary from yellow to greyish or dirty offwhite. There is a gradual transition, about three years, from the mottled brown of very young birds to a white plumage lightly dusted with brown specks, until the clear white and black plumage develops in mature birds.

Distribution: Common along the south western Cape coast, in estuaries and on vleis that are not too far inland. Also found near town rubbish dumps. Will follow ships as far as one hundred kilometres from shore in order to feed on rubbish thrown overboard. Breed on off-shore islands and at Swartklip and Rondevlei during spring and early summer, especially in October.

Notes: The favoured food of the Kelp Gull is the Donax sand mussel found in shallow water. It will fly up as much as fifteen metres and drop it to crack the shell. Offal

and other shell fish are also part of the diet and eggs and chicks are plundered from other sea birds. Nests, a scrape in the soil lined with grass, feathers or twigs, are to be found near some protective rock or plant, containing two or three eggs varying in colour from light green to turquoise or ochre, with dark markings. Apart from breeding on off-shore islands, as mentioned, nests are sometimes found on unfrequented cliffs or flats. In Afrikaans: Swartrug-meeu, in Xhosa: ama-Ngabongaba.

120. Greyheaded Gull *Larus cirrocephalus* 43 cm R288

Field Identification: The name is derived from the fact that during the breeding season the whole head is grey as seen in the photograph. When non-breeding the head is white but this species is then distinguished from Hartlaub's Gull by the fact that the bill is red with a blackish tip, and the eyes a light greyish red-rimmed yellow. Inner primaries are white as are the nape, throat, chest and belly. The upper wingspan is grey with outer primaries black, with a white spot near the tip. Legs are a dull red. The female is similar and young birds have irregular brownish markings and no white spot on primaries, yellow bills and brown legs.

Distribution: This is a fresh water gull found on large lakes and dams. Seen fairly regularly but nevertheless still considered an uncommon visitor to the south western Cape from further north. On rare occasions it has bred in the Bredasdorp District. A bird ringed in the Transvaal has been recovered at Gordon's Bay.

Notes: This species breeds with Hartlaub's Gull and a single bird has been recorded apparently breeding in a colony of Silver Gulls on Robben Island. Breeding takes place from July to November, when from two to three eggs are laid in a nest of dried grass, although sometimes old coots' nests are used. Considered a fairly tame bird. Makes a considerable noise at the nesting site that can be likened to a hysterical cackling. In Afrikaans: Gryskop-meeu.

121. Hartlaub's Gull *Larus hartlaubii* 38 cm R289

Field Identification: Very similar to the Greyheaded Gull but whereas the head of the latter species is entirely grey during the breeding season that of Hartlaub's Gull remains white down to the nape, upper parts grey, rump and tail white, wings black tipped. The neck, chest and underparts are white, the bill a dark reddish black. Certain individual birds develop a pale lavender ring around the neck during the breeding season. Eyes are brown with red eyelids, legs and webbed feet are dark red during the breeding season but black when non-breeding.

Distribution: Prolific on the west coast but not so abundant east of False Bay. During the winter months especially this species is to be found at inland vleis near Cape Town and follows trawlers up to 20 kms offshore. Will also frequent market places and rubbish dumps.

Notes: A noisy gregarious species allowing one to approach fairly close and not particularly shy. In 1974 some of these gulls were found breeding on the roof of the Somerset Hospital in Cape Town. Breed chiefly on islands off the west coast from April to September. Nests are constructed on the ground from bits of twigs, grasses and sometimes snail shells. The eggs are a light greenish brown with darker brown markings. The voice is a loud 'kwarrk' or a 'kek-kek-kek' at the breeding ground. In Afrikaans: Sterretjie.

122. Caspian Tern *Hydroprogne caspia* 56 cm R290

Field Identification: A beautiful glossy bird, the largest of the terns. When non-breeding the Caspian Tern has crown streaked with white, but when breeding, as in the photograph, there is a black cap effect over the eyes, the crown and down to the nape, with a strip over the bill and the sides of the face white. Throat, chest and underparts are white, rest of upperparts grey. The tail feathers are tipped with black, feet and legs are black, eyes reddish brown, bill red with a black tip. Nestlings are a dirty grey and young birds are barred and mottled with blackish brown above, and the tips of the tail feathers are barred.
Distribution: Resident along the coast and breeds in summer on some of the guano islands, at Reniers Kraal, Bredasdorp and at Strandfontein.
Notes: Gull-like in size and flight. Feeds on small fish and insects. The call is similar to the heron and is a raucous 'kraark'. Nests in large colonies but usually hunts for food singly or in pairs, often robbing other terns of their catch. Breeding time at the Cape is December and January, the nest being a scrape in the ground, lined with scraps, and containing two rough-textured greenish eggs marked with a few dark purple splotches. In Afrikaans: Reuse Seeswael.

123. Common Tern *Sterna hirundo* 33 cm R291

Field Identification: Generally seen here in non-breeding plumage since the Common Tern is a common non-breeding summer migrant to our coasts from the Palaearctic. The crown is usually a mottled black with sooty black over eye and on the back of the head; forehead, nape, throat and underparts white. Very pale grey above with a black bar on the shoulder of the wing, and the first primaries and outer tail feathers are black. Eyes are dark brown, legs dark reddish, the bill when non-breeding is black. When in breeding plumage the nape, crown and forehead are black, and the bill is red with a black tip. Females are the same and young birds resemble the non-breeding adult but upper parts are mottled grey and buff, bill reddish at base and legs yellowish.

Distribution: Present along the coast from August to April in great numbers but individuals may be found throughout the year, especially around estuaries where they roost on sandbanks. Often seen perching on boats in harbours. Ringed birds have been recovered from England, Norway, Finland, Denmark and Germany.
Notes: Often confused with the Arctic Tern. They have a buoyant swallow-like flight and are seen during the summer months in closely-packed masses on the shore or feeding in coastal waters. When the wings are folded the tail feathers do not extend beyond the wing tips which can be seen in the photograph. The sound they utter is a sharp screeching 'pee-err'. In Afrikaans: Gewone Seeswael.

124. Sandwich Tern *Sterna sandvicensis* 41 cm R296

Field Identification: A few characteristics distinguish this bird from other Terns, the most important being the yellow tip to the bill, which is evident from a considerable distance, but if this distance should be too great the tip may fade from view so that the remainder of the black bill appears shorter and stouter than that of other Terns. The tail is less deeply forked and the crown and nape feathers give a slightly crested appearance, well illustrated in the photograph. The wings and upper parts are a pale silvery grey, with neck, chest and underparts white. When non-breeding the crown and nape is mottled black, but, just before migrating at the end of summer, the forehead, crown and nape are black, and the underparts have a pinkish sheen. The female is similar. Eyes dark brown, bill black with yellow tip, legs black. Immature birds resemble non-breeding adults with rather more blackish markings.

Distribution: Found from August to April in the Cape in coastal waters, and present during those months in very large numbers. Many birds ringed at their European breeding grounds have been recovered in the Cape. A few birds stay during the winter months.
Notes: Exceptionally noisy birds occurring in flocks of many hundreds. When roosting at night their shrieking can be heard for hours, their call being a grating strident 'kirrik-kirrik'. In Afrikaans: Groot Seeswael.

125. Swift Tern *Sterna bergii* 49 cm R298

Field Identification: Mainly grey with long pointed wings. Forehead strip, sides of face, neck and underparts white, black legs and feet with yellow soles, large slightly curved yellow bill, often tinged with green at the base, eyes brown. In non-breeding plumage there is a white band above the bill, the crown is mottled black and white and there is a blackish bar on the shoulder. In breeding plumage, seen in the illustration of the Swift Tern with an egg, the white band above the bill persists, but the crown and nape are plain black. The sexes are alike and young birds resemble the non-breeding adult, but the mottling extends over the back and wings, and the primaries and tail feathers are blackish.
Distribution: Common in the south western Cape and to be found usually in small parties along the coast, or at estuaries. Socially inclined they form flocks of up to fifty birds, or associate with gulls and other terns. A bird ringed on Robben Island was recovered in Zululand. Breed on Schaapen, Marcus, Dyer, Malgas, Meeuw and Rob-

ben Islands from February to October, but not on each island every year. Also found on an island on the Strandfontein Sewage Works.

Notes: Graceful birds in flight due to the shape of the long gracefully pointed wings and high quick wing action. Colonial nesters often in association with Silver Gulls.

The nest is a shallow hollow lined with a little grass, containing one or two eggs with a basic colour of offwhite, as seen in the photograph, or light turquoise, or pale pink-ish, marked with brown splotches. The Swift Tern feeds on small fish and utters a raucous screaming 'kree-kree'. Seen sitting high up on masts and diving into the sea for food. In Afrikaans: Geelbek-seeswael.

126. Whitewinged Black Tern
Chlidonias leucopterus **23 cm R304**

Field Identification: As with other Terns there is a distinct difference between the non-breeding and breeding plumage. A distinguishing feature of this species, in common with the Whiskered Tern, is the square tail. When non-breeding the fore-head, forecrown and hind neck (forming a back collar) are white, with upper crown and nape mottled black and white. There is a blackish patch behind the eye and a blackish bar on the wing shoulder, with wings grey. Eyes are dark brown, bill black, legs orange-red. The photograph shows the Whitewinged Black Tern in breeding plumage with the whole head, nape, throat and underparts black but the bill, which turns crimson, has only a hint of crimson at the base. Wings are grey, with wing shoulder and tail white. The sexes are the same and young birds are darker and more mottled above, with flight and tail feathers tipped with offwhite. Towards the end of summer, before migrating, this species may be seen in partial breeding plum-age.

Distribution: A common non-breeding summer migrant from the Palaearctic, found at both permanent and temporary vleis or flooded fields.

Notes: Characteristically seen skimming over inland water looking for insects and

similarly over grasslands. They feed on a variety of insects, butterflies, worms and small fish. Usually found in small flocks but where conditions are very favourable, and food plentiful, flocks of around two thousand birds occur. The sound they utter is a rattling 'kerr'. In Afrikaans: Witvlerk-swartswael.

127. Whiskered Tern *Chlidonias hybridus* 24 cm R305

Field Identification: Often confused with the Whitewinged Black Tern when non-breeding, but there is no white collar on the hind neck, the bill appears larger, and the general plumage is slightly lighter grey. A black line extends through the eye, the crown is mottled black and white, the nape is black, otherwise this species is grey

110

above and white below. Eyes reddish brown, legs crimson, bill black but red when breeding. The illustration shows the Whiskered Tern in breeding plumage when the head is black from the bill, over the crown, and to the nape. The upper wing-coverts are dark, under wing-coverts light, chin and throat lightish grey, rump grey, chest and belly dark sooty grey. The sexes are similar and immature birds resemble the non-breeding adult but are mottled on mantle and back.

Distribution: The Whiskered Tern has bred irregularly in the south western Cape, but nevertheless with increasing frequency, at Verloren Vlei, at Paarl, in the Bredasdorp District, at Faure, and at Philippi.

Notes: Has similar feeding habits to the previous species but is more prone to feed by diving a metre or two into water for aquatic insects, in addition to which the frog *Hyperolius* is also eaten. Breeds from October to December, especially in November. As can be seen in the photograph the nest is constructed from dry grass placed in reeds, or on old nest. Eggs number two or three and are creamy coloured, occasionally washed with a tinge of green, and marked with dark brownish splotches. In Afrikaans: Witbaard-meerswael.

128. Namaqua Sandgrouse *Pterocles namaqua* 28 cm R307

Field Identification: Male and female need separate descriptions as with all the Sandgrouse family they are dissimilar, the male being the more outstanding in colouring of the two. This species is distinguished from other Sandgrouse by the long dark pointed tail. The male has head, neck, upper mantle and upper chest khaki gold, with a distinctive white bar across the chest slightly tinged above with lavender. The white bar is edged with a dark rufus band below and the lower chest and belly are a rich rufus. The plumage on the wings is dusky brown edged with white giving a crescent effect on the shoulder, with dark tips to the wings. Eyes brown, the short bill slate, the legs feathered down to the lavender grey toes. The female is streaked from the bill over the crown and nape with black, the throat is less streaked while the rest of the body and wings are mottled and barred with black, chestnut and buff. Young birds are mottled above, buff below, with lower belly blackish. As can be seen from the illustrations the general colouring of Sandgrouse is an effective camouflage for these ground-living birds.

Distribution: Near Cape Town and in the Hottentots Holland there are rare stragglers, but this species becomes more common in the dry northern and western areas. Recorded breeding at D.F. Malan Airport.

♀

Notes: Namaqua Sandgrouse fly very great distances from the dry western areas to visit water-holes. The male has chest feathers especially adapted to carry water for the young birds in the nest. They gather in their hundreds or even thousands at waterholes in the morning and become prey to Africans or Europeans, as they are excellent game birds, though perhaps a little tough. The flight is rapid and rather dove-like and they have a characteristic twist and turn as they glide down to the water. Their call on the wing is 'kelkiewyn'. Nests are a grass-lined scrape with usually three buff or grey eggs with red-brown and slate markings. In Afrikaans: Kelkiewyn.

129. Speckled Rock Pigeon *Columba guinea* 33 cm R311

Field Identification: The entire head is pearly grey with a red patch around the eyes, the neck pinkish chestnut with tips of feathers grey. The grey tipped wings are pinky chestnut with white speckles, the rump and tail darker grey, the latter having a wide black terminal band, underparts pearly grey. The bill is black, cere blue-grey, legs crimson. Females are similar but are usually not as bright in colour and are slightly smaller. Young birds lack the red on the face and have spots on wings brownish.

Distribution: Resident in the south western Cape and fairly common in Cape Town suburbs, sometimes nesting in tall palm trees. To be found on all rocky mountains, on islands off the west coast, and at newly ploughed grain fields.

Notes: Fast high flyers that will clap their wings in flight as a display during the courtship season. Large flocks can cause serious damage to grain crops and these

birds become targets for farmers. During the breeding season, which can be at al-most any time of the year, they will be seen in pairs. Usually lay two glossy white eggs found in a platform of sticks and roots on a ledge of rock, or even on a tall build-ing, less often in trees. Feed mainly on grain and also seeds of the Tribulus (duiwel-tjie-doring). The call is a rising and falling 'doo-doo-doo-doo'. In Afrikaans: Bosduif, in Zulu and Xhosa: i-Vukutu, in Sotho: le-Evakhotho.

130. Rameron Pigeon *Columba arquatrix* 40 cm R312

Field Identification: Forehead dark grey, crown lighter grey, throat, neck and nape mottled dark and light grey. The bare skin around the greyish yellow eyes is a bright yellow. The upper chest and mantle are grey tinged with maroon, the wing shoulders a deep greyish maroon with the for-ward section and chest spotted with white. The remainder of the wings, rump and tail are a deep bluish grey, underparts lighter grey, legs yellow. Females are slightly duller in colouring and a little smaller in size.

Distribution: Resident in the south western Cape and to be found in the berry bearing in-digenous forest areas.

Notes: Feed on berries, wild fruits and seeds found in the forested areas which they inhabit. They

113

are also very partial to olives which has caused them to be dubbed 'olive pigeons'. Inhabit the tops of tall trees and are not keen to leave that position unless for the purpose of drinking water at some nearby stream or pool. When not breeding they form quite large flocks. Very strong fliers. The call is a low rough 'coo'. Nests containing one glossy white egg are found, from November to February, in trees bordering the forest area. In Afrikaans: Geelbek-bosduif, in Xhosa: Izuba, in Zulu: i-Vugute, in Sotho: le-Phepane.

131. Redeyed Dove *Streptopelia semitorquata* 36 cm R314

Field Identification: The entire head, neck, chest and underparts are a light pinky grey highlighted by a fairly broad black band around the back of the neck and red rimmed eyes. The mantle and upper wing shoulder is often a sandy grey, with the rest of the wing a darker slate grey. Under tail-coverts grey, rump lightish sandy grey, dark grey tail feathers terminate with a broad light greyish brown band. Bill slaty black, legs greyish purple. The female resembles the male and young birds lack the black collar.

Distribution: Found at tree-enclosed rivers hitherto mainly in the more eastern parts of the south western Cape but now increasing in the vicinity of Cape Town. This species has reached west to Darling and Vredendal.

Notes: A sluggish bird found in thornveld and at forest rivers feeding on berries, seeds, fruits, tubers and termites. Spends most of its time high up in the trees but will descend to the ground periodically in search for food. During the courtship period it will display by ascending vigorously and descending in stages with rigid wings. Breeds from September to April, laying two white eggs in a nest constructed in a bush, a creeper or a tree. The call is a series of 'coos' with the fourth utterance stressed. In Afrikaans: Groot Ringduif, in Xhosa: Umakhulu, in Zulu: i-Hope.

132. Cape Turtle Dove *Streptopelia capicola* 28 cm R316

Field Identification: Distinguishing marks on the Cape Turtle Dove are the black half collar on the hind part of the neck and white tips to the outer tail feathers in flight. In other respects it greatly resembles the Laughing Dove. The head is grey, upper flight feathers beige with the underside bluish slate. Tail feathers grey, under tail-coverts white, chest and underparts pale grey. Eyes are black, legs purplish red, bill blackish grey. The female is the same and young birds are duller and have light edges to the plumage giving a mottled effect.

Distribution: This species is common and abundant wherever there are trees throughout the area – at tree-enclosed rivers, in the scrub forests on the southern

coast, in the Karoo and the Strandveld areas, the coastal Fynbos, mixed woodlands, pine forests, Rooikranz or Port Jackson plantations, in farmyards and in urban gardens or parks.

Notes: This is probably the most common dove, living in trees everywhere, and seen wandering about on the ground, bobbing its head with each step, in search of food. Lives on seeds particularly of the Euphorbia if available. Prefers to eat off the ground but will take seed from a table or birdbath. Breeds throughout the year laying two pure white eggs in a nest constructed in a tree by the female, with sticks brought to her by the male. The picture with two nestlings in the nest shows the nest of sticks which is progressively consolidated by the chicks faeces as they turn round in the nest. This phenomenon acts to hold together the original rather loose bundle of sticks and strengthen the whole construction as the chicks grow larger. Their very familiar call is 'coor-coor-coo' with accent on the middle syllable, sometimes described as 'How's father?' or 'Werk stadig'. In Afrikaans: Tortelduif, in Zulu: i-Hope, in Xhosa: Ihobe.

133. Laughing Dove *Streptopelia senegalensis* 25 cm R317

Field Identification: Similar to the Turtle Dove but without the black half collar and with a distinctive speckled reddish marking on the upper chest, brighter in the male bird. Head, neck and chest are a pinky greyish lilac, upper flight feathers rusty

beige, showing a great deal of the slate blue of the under-wing coverts. Belly and under-tail coverts are very pale greyish white, tail grey. The sexes are alike but the female is a little duller in colour, eyes dark brown, bill black, legs purplish red. Young birds lack speckled markings on chest and are generally more dullish brown.

Distribution: Very common and present in all treed areas, as is the Cape Turtle Dove, but more numerous in cultivated areas and less so in the wild. Mostly sedentary but a bird ringed at Rondevlei was recovered at Citrusdal and another at Kleinmond.

Notes: Rather smaller than the Cape Turtle Dove and common in gardens throughout the south west Cape, spending much of its time looking for weedseeds as it walks around with characteristic short steps. Feeds on grain crops as well and occasionally on insects. The voice of the Laughing Dove is a gentle descending cadence of notes 'cooroocoo-co-coo-coo'. Lays eggs at any time throughout the year, usually two, in a flimsy nest constructed in a tree. The eggs are white and glossy and the incubation is by both the male and female. The young leave the nest very early and are often picked up by people who think they have fallen out too soon, when in fact they should be left where they are found. In Afrikaans: Rooibors-duifie, in Sotho: le-Evakoko, in Zulu: u-Nonkenke.

134. Namaqua Dove *Oena capensis* 27 cm R318

Field Identification: The black face, throat and chest, and the long thin black tail distinguish this rather small dove from other species. The crown, sides of head and neck are greyish white merging into the soft mink brown of the mantle and wings. There are two dark bands, with a light band between, across the lower back, the rump is light beigy brown, underparts palest grey. The wing when folded shows two dark spots. The female does not have the black on face, throat and chest but is pale grey on forehead and throat, with crown and upper chest light cinnamon brown, bill blackish. Both male and female have eyes brown, legs purple; the male has bill purple at the base and the tip reddish orange. Young birds are barred below and have upper parts mottled buff, white, and black.

Distribution: Common in the Strandveld and Coastal Renosterbosveld areas and fairly widely distributed in the open country of the south western Cape but fairly rare in the Stellenbosch and Somerset West areas. Frequent dry areas and in such places are seen gathering at drinking places during the heat of the day.
Notes: Typically seen walking in a rather hunched-up way on the ground looking for food and seldom perched at any great height, choosing instead low fences or bushes. Fly at great speed showing the chestnut colouring in the wings, and characteristically raising and slowly lowering the long pointed tail on alighting. The nests built

by this species are rather more solid than those built by other doves and are found low down in bushes. Eggs are a creamy pale yellow and rather pointed in shape. They are laid at any time of the year with usually two in a clutch. Feed on small seeds and the call is an explosive 'twoo' followed by a softer 'hooo'. In Afrikaans: Namakwa-duifie, in Zulu: i-Gomboza, in Xhosa: isi-Vukazana, in Sotho: le-Evana-khoroana.

135. Cinnamon Dove *Aplopelia larvata* 27 cm R322

Field Identification: An extremely beautiful and colourful bird, unlikely to be confused with any other dove. The forehead, sides of face and throat are white, the crown, nape, mantle and upper chest an iridescent mixture of bronzy green and cinnamon pink, underparts cinnamon, upper parts a mixture of russet brown and green. The female is similar and young birds have dirty white faces, no metallic sheen, and are more rufous brown.

Distribution: Found only in indigenous forest from Cape Town eastwards along the coastal regions. Difficult to see as this species usually sits motionless on the ground under evergreen trees and are quiet and wary.

Notes: Live on berries and seeds as well as tiny insects. There is a typical back and forth movement of the head as it utters a low 'hoo-oo' and a further call is a squeak uttered as many as thirty times with three second intervals. The tail is held high when walking on the ground and if disturbed the Cinnamon Dove will fly off noisily, perch low in the undergrowth and usually return to the same spot to continue feeding. Two creamy yellow eggs are laid in a nest just above the ground either in a low bush or in matted creepers. The illustration shows the Cinnamon Dove on the nest made of sticks with two very tiny newly-hatched chicks just visible in the front. In Afrikaans: Kaneel-duifie.

136. Redchested Cuckoo *Cuculus solitarius* 30 cm R343

Field Identification: The well known 'Piet-my-vrou', easily identified by the chestnut-red upper chest, and black bars on buff lower chest and belly. Head, nape, and back are grey, upper wings darker grey, under wings barred with white, underparts buff. The long, full, rounded tail is blackish grey sparsely spotted with white down the centre and round the edge. Eyes dark reddish brown edged with yellow, bill black above and yellowish below, legs yellow. The female is paler and young birds are a mottled black and white above and there is no red on the chest.

Distribution: Common throughout the area except on the dry west side of the Peninsula north of Hout Bay. A breeding summer migrant arriving in September and leaving again in March, some over-wintering.

Notes: Parasitic on the Cape Robin, the Cape Rock Thrush and the Cape Wagtail. The Redchested Cuckoo deposits its egg in the nest of one of these species and when the chick is hatched it ejects the other eggs from the nest. The egg is a shiny brown or olivy green sometimes marked with a reddish brown. This species is found perched in thickly foliaged trees and utters a loud ringing 'ship-whip-wheeoo' commonly said to be 'Piet-my-vrou'. During summer this call is uttered incessantly even during the hours of the night but over-wintering birds are silent. Feeds mainly on grubs, caterpillars and beetles. In Afrikaans: Piet-my-vrou, in Zulu: Pezukomkono, in Xhosa: Uphezukomkhono.

137. Klaas's Cuckoo *Chrysococcyx klaas* 18 cm R351

Field Identification: Fairly similar to the Didric Cuckoo but there are not the same distinct white spots on the tail or wing plumage. The male is an iridescent bright green with a touch of bronze on the shoulder. The centre of the neck and chest is white, with brown and white bars on the lower belly, tail green with outer feathers white. Eyes brown, bill greenish brown with the curved tip black, legs olivy grey. The female is illustrated in the photograph. The head is buff barred with brown; throat, chest, and underparts whitish barred with brown. Upper parts are brownish barred with bronze,

the wing shoulder bright green barred with bronze. Tail feathers green and brown, with outer feathers white. Sometimes the female resembles the male. Distinguishing marks on immature birds are white ear patches and black beaks.

Distribution: Occurs all the year round but unless uttering its call is rather an inconspicuous migrant which is easily overlooked. A common species of the grasslands and rocky hills near the coast, seen mainly in winter, the female being seen less often than the male.

Notes: This species is named in honour of le Vaillant's faithful Hottentot servant, Klaas. Parasitises various fly-catchers and sunbirds, particularly the Apalis in October and November. The photograph shows a Klaas's Cuckoo Chick having hatched in a Cape Batis nest after being deposited there by the parent bird. Eggs are very varied in colour and are laid during the period from October to March in the nest of the host. When hatched the chicks eject the young of the host. Klaas's Cuckoo lives on a wide variety of insects and caterpillars. The male is the noisier of the two sexes and utters a repeated 'whit jeh', referred to in Afrikaans as 'Meitjie', which is a good representation of the call and which is the Afrikaans name for this species.

138. Didric Cuckoo *Chrysococcyx caprius* 20 cm R352

Field Identification: Upper parts iridescent green shot with bronze (particularly on mantle and shoulders) and gold. There is a strong white mark behind the eye with a black line running through the eye area, and further white markings in front of the eye and on the crown, eyes dark red. Throat, sides of neck and upper chest white, belly and lower parts white barred with greenish black. The wing tips and tail plumage are a darker iridescent greenish grey, and there is a liberal white spotting on the outer tail feathers and along the wing plumage. Bill black, legs blackish grey. Females are duller with barring on chest and sides of neck as well. Immature birds are iridescent green or chestnut brown barred with green above, and are heavily marked with green below, bill coral red.

Distribution: A migrant parasitising the Cape Sparrow, weavers, and, in the more northern and eastern areas, the Red Bishop.

Notes: This species is still considered fairly rare in the area but increasing. Feed on hairy caterpillars and insects. The call is a plaintive 'dee-dee-deederik' answered by the female with a 'deea-deea-deea'. During the breeding season males establish their own territories and noisily defend their rights, calling the females which come to them for mating. Males also fly with tails outspread for display, calling loudly. The female will fly to the nest of the host bird when she is about to lay her egg and deposit it with great speed. After hatching, the cuckoo chick will eject the eggs or young of the host bird. In Afrikaans: Diedrikkie.

139. Whitebrowed Coucal
Centropus supercilliosus burchellii 40 cm R356

Field Identification: The light eyebrows and upper tail-coverts barred in very dark greenish brown and buff distinguish this species. The sides and top of the head are a glossy black with white stripes on back of head and mantle, back chestnut brown with light white stripes. The short rounded wings are chestnut, eyes red, bill black, legs blackish grey, tail feathers glossy black tipped with a thin offwhite bar. The female is similar and young birds have head and nape a dull black, and sides, back, and tail feathers barred.

Distribution: Resident on vleis, marshes, in reed beds and along tree lined rivers. Well established at Zeekoe Vlei and at Hout Bay.

Notes: The commonest coucal in South Africa, popularly known as the 'rain bird'. Seen singly or in pairs and more evident during the breeding season, at which time it is more likely to come out into the open from its usual haunts in reed beds and in scrub near streams, rivers and dams. Flies heavily to the next cover and feeds on grasshoppers, insects or small animals such as mice. The call is one of the most characteristic sounds of South Africa and is a series of flutelike notes sounding like 'doo-doo-doo-doo', uttered about seventeen times as descending notes and rising at the end. Also utters a harsher alarm call like 'kek-kek-kek-kek' repeated many times.

The nest is formed from an untidy heap of grass blades lined with green leaves, placed about three metres from the ground in a tree or bush. Breeding time is from September to February. Eggs number from three to five and are white in colour. Chicks leave the nest at about twenty days and clamber about in the bush defecating a foul-smelling liquid if threatened. In Afrikaans: Vleiloerie, in Xhosa: Ubikhwe, in Sotho: Makhofe, in Zulu: u-Fookwe.

140. Barn Owl *Tyto alba* 33 cm R359

Field Identification: The pointed offwhite heart-shaped facial disc outlined with golden buff is the most characteristic identification as well as the fact that there are no ear-tufts. Golden buff above and on upper chest, speckled with grey. Tail and wing feathers are barred in dusky. Lighter buff on belly also speckled with grey, and offwhite below spotted with brown. The female is similar and young birds are darker grey above and washed with buff below. Eyes dark brown, hooked bill horn, legs yellowy flesh.

Distribution: Resident in cultivated areas throughout the area. Found in quiet nooks in buildings, in holes in trees, in open lofts and in dark caves, nevertheless fairly rare.

Notes: Breeding takes place from March to September and eggs are laid on ledges, on loft floors, and in disused Hamerkop nests. The eggs are white and number five to nine. The Barn Owl is an invaluable asset as over eighty percent of its food consists of rodents – birds forming part of the diet during spring. Hunts in the dark of night, or, occasionally, on very overcast days, looking pale and ghostly by moonlight. Makes eerie screaming and snoring noises which are probably responsible for some of the superstitions surrounding this bird – one being that there will be a death in the house if a Barn Owl utters a call on the roof. In Afrikaans: Nonnetjie-uil, in Sotho: Sephooko, in Xhosa: Isikhova.

141. Grass Owl *Tyto capensis* 35 cm R360

Field Identification: A larger owl than the Barn Owl, the darker crown, head and mantle giving a dark capped effect to the rounded heart-shaped face. The facial disc is buff, edged with white and dark colouring around the black eyes make them appear large. Upper parts are brown flecked with white, the chest is yellow flecked with brown, belly and underparts pale beige lightly spotted with brown or black. The brownish tail is not barred and there are no ear-tufts. The hooked bill is horn and the legs yellow. Females are similar and immature birds are more golden.

Distribution: A fairly rare species but resident at marshes and vleis.

Notes: The Grass Owl lives in long grass near streams or vleis and less frequently in lightly wooded areas, but does not perch in trees, preferring to sit on the ground. Will fly short distances and drop into the grass once more. Food is derived mainly from rodents, the longer bill suggesting that its prey is larger than that of the Barn Owl. Three to five white eggs are laid from October to February, occasionally in May. The young of one brood may vary considerably in size. In Afrikaans: Grasuil, in Xhosa: Isikhova.

142. Marsh Owl *Asio capensis* 36 cm R361

Field Identification: Large blackish rings surrounding the eyes and short ear tufts distinguish this from other owl species. The round facial disc is pale beige, brown above, chest pale beige finely speckled with brown, belly beige with crescent-shaped brown markings, secondaries and tail broadly barred in brown and offwhite. The sexes are the same and young birds are a deeper shade than adult birds. Eyes brown, bill black, legs yellowish flesh.

Distribution: More common in the south western Cape than the Grass Owl but resident in similar habitats around marshes and vleis.

Notes: The best time to spot Marsh Owls is just before sunset when they are to be seen flying around the areas they inhabit. During the day they are usually hidden in the long grass in marshy ground where they feed on frogs, lizards, insects, small birds and mice. There are two breeding seasons, from July to August, or from March to April. Three or four rounded white eggs are laid. The call is a croak similar to that made by a frog and it is uttered in flight. In Afrikaans: Vlei-uil.

143. Wood Owl *Strix woodfordii* 34 cm R362

Field Identification: The delightful illustration is of the adult Wood Owl and a nestling. There are no ear tufts, the large brown eyes are highlighted by a circle of dark plumage which in turn is surrounded by white edged plumage. Throat, chest and belly are barred in brown and white, and the hooked bill is yellow, but red at the base. Individuals vary in ground colour from darkest brown to a deep russet. The head is speckled with white spots and there are large white spots on the central wing-coverts. Legs and feet are pinkish yellow. The sexes are similar, young birds are a lighter sandy beige, and nestlings are finely barred in brown and offwhite as seen in the photograph.

Distribution: Has adapted to living in some of the suburbs in Cape Town. Normally resident in dense bush or well forested areas.
Notes: Usually spotted on a branch of a tree close to the main trunk. Feeds on grasshoppers, crickets and caterpillars, occasionally taking small mice, birds and frogs. There has been one report of a Wood Owl attacking a snake. The call is said to be the Zulu equivalent of 'Oh my mother' and sounds like 'weh mameh' or 'who are you'. The nest is made in hollow logs and the same nest, usually about three metres from the ground, may be used year after year. One or two eggs, white in colour, are laid during the period from August to October. In Afrikaans: Bosuil, in Xhosa: i-Bengwana.

144. Spotted Eagle Owl *Bubo africanus* 45 cm R368

Field Identification: The commonest of the owls a distinguishing feature being the long eartufts. The general colour is a mottled greyish beige heavily speckled with black and white. There are definite white spots on the mantle. The wings and tail are broadly barred in blackish brown and white; finely barred below. The eyes vary from yellow to a golden orange and the bill and legs are black. Females are similar and immature birds have smoky barring on the head. The illustrations show an adult perched in a tree at night, and a charming lineup of nestlings.
Distribution: A sedentary species, very widely distributed throughout the entire area. Usually sighted early in the mornings or at dusk perched on a vantage point. Favours hilly bushy country but is found in open country as well.
Notes: The Spotted Eagle Owl sleeps during the day, emerging at sunset to hunt.

Feeds on rats, mice, lizards, moles, great numbers of insects and occasionally on birds. The call is a loud 'hu-hoo' the male call being in a higher register than that of the female. Nesting occurs mainly from September to October but could be during the longer period from July to December, also very occasionally in May. Nests containing two or three white eggs may be found in wells, on ledges in cliffs, on houses, in the hollow of trees or on the top of Hamerkop or Weaver's nests. In Afrikaans: Gevlekte Ooruil, in Zulu: isi-Kova, in Xhosa: Isihuluhulu.

Spotted Eagle Owl chicks

145. Fierynecked Nightjar *Caprimulgus pectoralis* 24 cm R373

Field Identification: Sometimes referred to as the South African Nightjar and distinguished by a distinct rufous collar on hind neck and broad black streaks on the centre of the crown, evident in the illustration. A medium-sized, long-winged bird with a very small greyish brown bill and large reddish brown eyes. There are large white spots on both sides of the neck, a white streak beneath the eyes and bright rufous on throat and chest – above and below the white on the front neck. The upper parts are barred and spotted in black, greyish buff and white – the overall effect being a 'dead bark' colouring which serves as an excellent camouflage during the day for this nocturnal species. The wing feathers are blackish, with the first four primaries spotted with white, and the central tail feathers are grey barred with black. The two outer tail feathers of the male bird are broadly tipped with white, more narrowly so in the case of the female. Legs and feet are dark brown and young birds are paler below.

Distribution: Resident and fairly common throughout the Cape, the call, described below, being a characteristic sound on moonlit nights, especially soon after sunset and shortly before the dawn.

Notes: Feeds at night, hunting from a definite perch and not ranging over a wide area. Catches a wide spectrum of insects while on the wing and favours the areas around gums and pine trees. As they do not venture from their shady hiding places during the day they are difficult to spot, but will sometimes be seen in the light of one's car headlight, hunting next to a country road. The call is a musical whistle with three syllables, like 'wheh-wheh-wheh', with the third syllable descending. Breeds from August to October with a peak in September, the eggs being laid on debris under the trees which they inhabit. There are usually two, salmon-pink with darker pink and brown markings. Will feign injury when endeavouring to protect their young. In Afrikaans: Afrikaanse Naguil, in Xhosa: Udebesa.

146. African Black Swift *Apus barbatus* 19 cm R380

(Illustration overleaf)

Field Identification: A smallish sooty black bird with a glossy black mantle, and upper wings slightly tinged with a greenish bronze. The eyes, tiny bill and sharp curved claws, with all four toes pointing forwards, are black. The throat is white, very finely streaked with black, underparts dark sooty black, underwings and under the forked tail sooty brown. The tail is less forked than in some other species of swifts. The female is similar and young birds have pale edges to the plumage, especially on the wings.

Distribution: They rarely settle and are, like all the Swifts, the most completely aerial of birds, impossible to photograph and illustrated here by paintings. A resident bird with no habitat preference and present throughout the area, departing again in March with odd stragglers left behind.

Notes: Feed on insects taken in flight and are common in large flocks at the cliffs where they breed in September, alighting momentarily or seen scuttling into their nests. Seen in the company of other Swift species especially when there is a surfeit of airborne insects. Two white eggs may be found in the crevice of a cliff, protected by some overhang. In Afrikaans: Swart Windswael, in Sotho: Lekhaqasi, in Xhosa: Ihlankomo.

147. Whiterumped Swift *Apus caffer* 15 cm R383

(Illustration overleaf)

Field Identification: A distinguishing feature in flight is the long deeply forked tail, and this species is blacker than the Little Swift. Slender scythe-like wings are blackish with edges of wing plumage, tail, and head, more sooty brown above. There is a short narrow white band across the black rump, visible only from above and not from the side. The throat is white, underparts sooty brown with a blue-black sheen, eyes and tiny bill black, feet dusky brown. In flight, and viewed from below, the only white to be seen is on the throat with underparts and the forward edge of the outstretched wings darker than the trailing edge of the wings and the tail. The female is similar and immature birds have flight feathers edged with white.

Distribution: A common summer migrant found within reach of mountainous areas and in towns. Breeds in the area in summer and there are many winter records.

Notes: Seen mainly in pairs or small parties and when not breeding will mix with other swifts. Has the usual fast direct flight common to Swifts and feeds on insects taken on the wing. The call is considered to be bat-like and consists of a low twittering. Is known to take over the nests of swallows or to nest under the eaves of buildings or in crevices in rocks. The nest is lined with some of the birds own feathers and from one to three white eggs are laid. In Afrikaans: Witkruis-windswael, in Xhosa: u-Nonqane.

148. Horus Swift *Apus horus* 16 cm R384

(Illustration overleaf)

Field Identification: A little larger and more heavily built than the Whiterumped Swift, the fork in the tail is wider but not as deep, and the white on the rump is more extensive. Top of head brown, upper wings and mantle brownish black, lower back and rump white, tail brownish black. Chin and throat white, sides of face, chest, belly and underparts brownish black, under tail and under wings smoky brown.

Eyes brown, small bill and feet dusky. Sexes similar, young birds more mottled.

Distribution: Breeds in the Bain's Kloof and recorded sightings at Ysterfontein, De Hoop and Paarl. Not as common as other Swift species, seen at sandbanks where they breed, not usually on crevices where other Swifts nest.

Notes: Seen arriving at the entrance to a metre-deep tunnel in a sandbank and vanishing rapidly, or leaving and flying away at great speed. Often occupy the old sandbank nests of Sand Martins, Bee-eaters or Ground Woodpeckers. The nest is at the end of the tunnel and would be up to 10 cm wide carpeted with fibres, feathers and bits of vegetable down, usually collected in flight. The eggs are white and number one to four, more often two or three. In Afrikaans: Horus-windswael.

149. Little Swift *Apus affinis* 14 cm R385

Field Identification: A small swift with only a very slight fork in the tail when held closed, giving a square outline, or fan-shaped when fully extended. Crown is whitish finely speckled with brown becoming more brown towards the nape, blackish brown over mantle and wings, except the trailing edges which are slightly lighter sooty brown. There is a broad white band across the rump with tail blackish brown at base and sooty brown at the tip. Chin and throat are white, underparts blackish brown, under wings and tail brown. Tiny bill black, eyes and feet brown.

Distribution: A breeding summer migrant which has expanded its range into the south western Cape in recent years. Some remain during winter. Mainly town dwelling, nesting in crevices in buildings or under overhanging ledges.

Notes: Flight pattern is more fluttering than other swifts with a less rapid and direct flight. Inclined to glide with wings held up vertically and tail fanned out. Nest on buildings, as described, or less often in rocky areas or under bridges, and gather round the nesting site twittering and shrieking shrilly at sunrise and sunset. Feed on insects taken in flight. Nests are made of feathers and straw, glued together with a regurgitated jelly-like saliva. Nests are sometimes isolated or may be side by side and overlapping. Eggs number two or three and are glossy white. In Afrikaans: Klein Windswael.

150. Alpine Swift *Apus melba* 22 cm R386

Field Identification: The largest of the Swifts present in the area distinguished in flight by the white belly separated from the white chin and throat by a broad brown breast band. Mouse brown above with a tinge of green, dark brown below with plumage on breast, sides and under tail-coverts edged with white. Under wings and under tail brown. Eyes and feet brown, small bill black. Sexes similar, young birds mottled below and with white edges to wing plumage.

Distribution: A mountain species, chiefly a summer migrant to these areas ranging for food far over the surrounding countryside. Undoubtedly breeds in the precipices of Table Mountain but nobody has ever recorded reaching the nests.

Notes: Utters a loud chittering call in flight. Mixes with other Swifts and Sand Martins and ranges far and wide having a powerful rapid flight pattern. Collects serial debris in flight, such as seeds, pieces of feather and bits of vegetable down to construct the nest which is glued together with a jelly-like regurgitated saliva. Nests in krantzes under rocky overhangs. In Afrikaans: Witpens-windswael, in Xhosa: Ubantom.

Horus Swift

African Black
Swift

Whiterumped
Swift

Little
Swift

Alphine Swift

130

151. Speckled Mousebird *Colius striatus* 30–35 cm R390

Field Identification: The appearance of a blackish face is gained from the bare black skin around the dark brown eyes and the fairly small black upper bill. The lower mandible is bluish white. This species has neither the red face of the Redfaced Mousebird nor white on the back like the Whitebacked Mousebird. The entire head and hair-like crest is greyish brown. The particular bird photographed here appears rather more brown than is usual, the more frequent colouring being throat blackish, breast buff finely barred with brown, underparts paler buff. The long tail feathers are brownish grey, upper parts ash brown with back and rump finely vermiculated, legs varying from darkish brown to dull red. Females are similar and young birds have the upper bill a bright yellowish green. This species has the outer toes reversible either backwards or forwards and the claws are strong and curved to aid climbing.

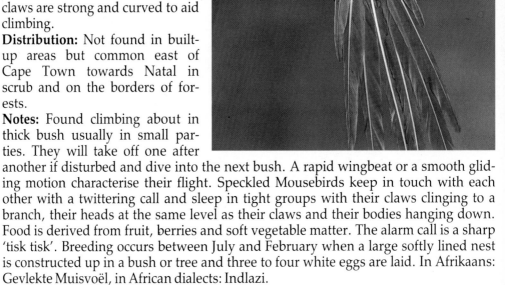

Distribution: Not found in built-up areas but common east of Cape Town towards Natal in scrub and on the borders of forests.

Notes: Found climbing about in thick bush usually in small parties. They will take off one after another if disturbed and dive into the next bush. A rapid wingbeat or a smooth gliding motion characterise their flight. Speckled Mousebirds keep in touch with each other with a twittering call and sleep in tight groups with their claws clinging to a branch, their heads at the same level as their claws and their bodies hanging down. Food is derived from fruit, berries and soft vegetable matter. The alarm call is a sharp 'tisk tisk'. Breeding occurs between July and February when a large softly lined nest is constructed up in a bush or tree and three to four white eggs are laid. In Afrikaans: Gevlekte Muisvoël, in African dialects: Indlazi.

152. Whitebacked Mousebird *Colius colius* 32 cm R391

Field Identification: One could describe this bird as a paler and greyer version of the previous species, the Speckled Mousebird, with a bluish white bill, reddish legs, black eyes, a white line down the centre of the back and a maroon red rump. Long tail feathers are greyish buff. Females are similar and young birds lack the red rump and have the upper bill a bright blue-green.

Distribution: Fairly common in the drier western areas becoming the rarest of the three Mousebird species east of the Hottentots Holland. Fairly generally distributed wherever there are fruit-bearing trees and bushes.

Notes: A sociable species usually seen in parties and sleeping in bunches like the previous species. Feeds on fruits and soft vegetable matter which is quite often found on the ground. The call is a pretty 'tzee-tzit-tzit' and an alarm is sounded with a sharp metallic 'tzik'. The breeding season is usually from September to October,

but there are single records of breeding in February, March, April and December. Nests are found between two and seven metres up in thick bushes. They are large cup-like structures made from dry sticks and lined with soft vegetable matter. The rough white eggs number three or four. In Afrikaans: Witkruis-muisvoël.

153. Redfaced Mousebird *Colius indicus* 33 cm R392

Field Identification: The photograph shows very clearly the contrast between the buffish brown of the throat, chest and underparts, giving an impression of a buffish brown bird when viewed from the front, and the greyish green of the upper parts, when viewed from the side or from above. The forehead is tinged with chestnut, the cere and upper mandible are crimson red, as is the bare skin surrounding the dark grey eyes. Tip of upper mandible and the lower mandible are black, legs red. The sexes are alike and young birds have the bare skin around the eyes, as well as the bill, a greenish colour.

Distribution: Fairly widely distributed throughout the area yet this species is the least numerous of the Mousebirds. Found wherever there are trees even in developed areas.

Notes: Sociable gregarious birds found in parties and often spotted flying in groups high overhead calling a clear 'tiu-woo-woo' or 'tree-ree-ree'. Breeds from September to February. The name Mousebird derives from the type of hairlike plumage, particularly on the crown, and the habit they have of 'crawling' around in the trees.

When alarmed they will, typically, crawl to the top of a tree and fly off one by one. The typical nest of the Mousebirds, made of sticks and high up in a tree, is shown in the illustration. The eggs are white scrolled with reddish brown. In Afrikaans: Rooiwang-muisvoël, in Xhosa: Intshili, in Zulu: um-Tshivovo.

154. Pied Kingfisher *Ceryle rudis* 29 cm R394

Field Identification: Unmistakable with the long pointed black beak running in line with the black stripe on the elongated head, giving an appearance of even greater length. There is a white eyebrow stripe which continues around the head, with the crown black, and the crest black or black and white. The photograph shows the male above and the female below. Throat, chest and belly are white, the male having two black bands of varying width on the upper chest, and the female having black markings on either side shaped almost like a rounded 'peter-pan' collar. Upper parts and wing feathers are black spotted or barred with white. Eyes are blackish brown, bill and legs black. Young have buff edges to white plumage.

Distribution: The commonest Kingfisher in the south western Cape widely distributed on fresh and salt water, on the coast at Cape Agulhas, and resident at rivers with rocky beds.

Notes: Hovers over the water beating its wings rapidly, body vertical and bill pointed down before diving to catch its prey, usually a fish, which is taken to a favourite perch and beaten to death before being eaten. Will also take flying insects, crabs and shrimps. Often seen alone or in pairs perched in exposed positions near water, characteristically raising and lowering the tail. Breeds from August to November, making its nest in a burrow in a bank and containing bones and fish scales from previous prey. Eggs number four to six and are white and glossy. This is a noisy bird uttering a call resembling a sharp 'kwik-wik'. In Afrikaans: Bont Visvanger, in Sotho: Seinoli, in xhosa: Isaxwila, in Zulu: isi-Quba.

155. Giant Kingfisher *Ceryle maxima* 44 cm R395

Field Identification: As the name would imply this is the largest of the Kingfishers with the very large pointed bill of the fish eater, the elongated head being typical of the Kingfishers. The male as seen in the photograph has crown, crest, sides of face, hind neck and upper parts black spotted with white. The throat is white and sides of neck white and black, chest bright chestnut, lower parts barred with black on white, tail black barred with white. The female, illustrated in the second photograph is similar above, but has throat and upper chest black with plumage edged with white and a broad white band across the middle of the chest separating the upper black and white from the deep chestnut of the belly and underparts. Eyes blackish brown, short legs olivy grey. Immature birds have the sides of chest a mixture of chestnut and black.

Distribution: Found along tree-lined rivers even those passing through the suburbs of Cape Town, but in general this species can not be considered as common as the Pied Kingfisher. Will not be found at bare dams without trees but frequents wooded areas around streams, lagoons and coastal pools.

Notes: Feeds on fish caught from a sheltered perch over or near water, usually diving straight from the perch into the water for its prey. The call is usually uttered in flight and is a loud clear 'kakh-kakh-kakh-kakh'. Often guilty of preying on goldfish kept in fish ponds. Breeding period is from September to January and three to four eggs will be found at the end of a long tunnel as long as one to three metres in depth burrowed in the bank alongside a stream. In Afrikaans: Reuse visvanger, in Xhosa: Uxomoyi, in Zulu: isi-Vuba.

♀

156. Halfcollared Kingfisher *Alcedo semitorquata* 20 cm R396

Field Identification: A fairly rare bird and the only blue Kingfisher with a long black beak. A white patch on the side of the neck forms the half collar, the chin is buff and the front neck white. The forehead and crown are striped with deep cobalt blue and an iridescent marina, sides of face, back of head, and nape, deep cobalt blue. Upper parts and tail are iridescent marina, lower back and rump greyish blue, tail tip deep cobalt blue. The wing shoulder is peacock green shot through with bronze and edged, along the forward edge, with bright spots of lighter peacock green, rest of wing plumage peacock green shot through with bronze. The breast has a large side patch of cobalt blue on the rich golden colour, which extends down to the belly and underparts. Eyes black, short legs and feet red. Females are similar and young birds have a slight black barring across the chest.

Distribution: Not common, in fact rare, throughout the south western Cape. Found perched low down next to large streams. Probably resident and breed in these tree-lined areas. Visits the coast and open vleis.

Notes: Has a quick bobbing action when agitated. Feeds on small fish, crabs, water animals and insects. The cry is a shrill repeated 'seep-seep'. Nests from September to November and in March. Three or four white eggs are laid at the end of a tunnel from one to three metres long, about 40 cm from the top of a sandbank, next to a stream. It will be fouled with droppings. In Afrikaans: Blou Visvanger. Two African names are: isi-Xwiba and Chinyurahowe.

157. Malachite Kingfisher *Alcedo cristata* 13 cm R397

Field Identification: A magnificently colourful species with forehead, sides of face, throat, chest and underparts rich golden cinnamon, chin white. The crested crown is a bright fluorescent marina striped with black, sides of head, nape, wings and upper parts, deep iridescent cobalt blue. There is a white mark on either side of the hind neck. Underwings dusky and the tail, typically short like all the kingfishers, cobalt blue above and golden cinnamon below. The long pointed bill is bright red, black at the base, eyes dark brown, legs coral. The female is the same and young birds have black bills, backs black mottled with green.

Distribution: Common in fresh water situations such as streams and marshes where there is sheltering vegetation, and occasionally on rock pools along the coast.

Notes: Breeding time for this small colourful Kingfisher is from September to February, the nest being an odorous space at the end of a tunnel in a river bank, filled with the remains of fish and insects. Eggs number three to five and are glossy white. Finds a perch overlooking water and dives for its prey, skimming low over the water to another perch if alarmed, uttering a shrill 'peep-peep'. Feeds on tiny fish, tadpoles, shrimps, beetles and grasshoppers. Inclined to turn its head and turn round very quickly on its perch and has a characteristic way of moving its crest sideways when raised. In Afrikaans: Kuifkop-visvanger, in Xhosa: in-Dozela, or Isaxinila.

158. Brownhooded Kingfisher *Halcyon albiventris* 24 cm R402

Field Identification: Dark streaks on the light flanks are a distinguishing feature. Head, sides of neck and nape are ash streaked with black, giving the hooded appearance and leaving a light eyebrow and neck; chin white, chest washed with chestnut.

The mantle, scapulars and wing-coverts are black, tail and edges of flight feathers deep marina blue. The large pointed bill is dull red, tipped with black, eyes dark brown, legs dark reddish black. Females are brown instead of black on mantle and scapulars, young birds have black bills, slightly red at the base, and are streaked below.

Distribution: Considered rare in the south western Cape. An inhabitant of Swellendam, Bonnievale, Hermanus and Riviersonderend. Recorded once in Rosebank in Cape Town, once near Wellington and Rawsonville, and several times in the Du Toits Kloof. More commonly found east of Cape Town along the Cape coast towards Natal. Sometimes found in gardens.

Notes: An insectiverous kingfisher often found far away from water. Lives on a wide range of food including beetles, grasshoppers, crabs, lizards, small mice or snakes and young birds. The breeding time is from September to December when it burrows into a sandbank for about a metre and makes an enlarged area at the end for a nest. The whole burrow becomes foul with droppings, bits of insects and maggots. Four or five white eggs are laid. Characteristically bobs up and down, particularly before flying off when disturbed. Males display when courting by parading to and fro and spreading their wings. The cry is a noisy 'kik-kik-kik-kik' on a slightly descending pitch. In Afrikaans: Bruinkop-visvanger, in Xhosa: Undozela, in Zulu: u-Nongozolo.

137

159. European Bee-eater *Merops apiaster* 27 cm R404

Field Identification: Like all Bee-eaters a very colourful attractive bird with a fairly long, slender slightly curved bill. Crown, nape, back and wing-coverts cinnamon, with a black stripe through the eye from the bill, and a thin black half collar round the front of the throat, under the yellow chin. The forehead is yellow in the centre and greenish above the eyes; chest, belly and underparts turquoise green. Rump and scapulars bronzy yellow, flight feathers turquoise green. Tail deep greyish green, with central tail feathers elongated. Eyes red, bill black, legs greyish. The sexes are the same, immature birds have green on nape, back, and rump, the collar is faint and the central tail feathers are not elongated.

Distribution: Usually arrives in the Cape about October and leaves in February. Thought to be declining in numbers. A rare straggler in the southern and eastern parts of the south western Cape, becoming more common and breeding from Darling northwards.

Notes: Often identified by their call – a lovely clear 'kiwirry' as a flock circle high up in the sky. Prey on bees, wasps, grasshoppers, dragonflies, butterflies and termites. Nest in holes in banks from September to December, laying four to six white eggs. In Afrikaans: Europese Byvreter, in Sotho: Thlapolome.

160. Bluecheeked Bee-eater *Merops persicus* 30 cm R406

Field Identification: Distinguished from the European Bee-eater by its green back and from Boehm's Bee-eater by the lighter eyebrow marking and bluish-white cheek. General colour above and below brown-tinged olive green. As with all the bee-eaters there is a black mark through the eye and the Bluecheeked Bee-eater has a white and blue eyebrow stripe with a light stripe below the eye as well. throat cinnamon, tail, with central feathers slightly elongated, greyish green; eyes red, bill black, legs brownish.

Distribution: The photograph was taken at Klawervlei, where seven individuals were present from January to the end of March. They arrived in early stages of breeding plumage and were seen to feed mainly on dragonflies, sleeping in the willows. This race closely resembles the Madagascar race. Other sightings have been made at Hermanus, Kuils River and the Cape Flats.

Notes: A rare migrant to Africa from Persia and Malagasy usually seen during the period from September to April wheeling about in flocks near their roosts in mangrove swamps or in reed beds; a rare periodic migrant to the south western Cape. Feeds on flying insects such as bees, dragonflies and termites. Has a clear call similar to that of the European Bee-eater. Breeds in colonies laying three or more white eggs in a hole drilled in a bank. Known to breed in Rhodesia. In Afrikaans: Blouwang-byvreter.

161. Hoopoe *Upupa epops* 27 cm R418

Field Identification: Identified immediately by the rather spectacular long erect brick-red crest, tipped and spotted with black. The head, neck, throat, chest and mantle are a similar colour, in striking contrast to the black and white barring on the wing and tail feathers, with primaries black. The lower back is barred with pale tan and black and the tail plumage has a wide black terminal band. Underparts light tan, eyes dark brown, long pointed bill blackish towards the tip and lighter towards the base, legs greyish black. The female is smaller and duller in colour, the young are a dirty brown with secondaries barred with black and white.
Distribution: Resident and common in the south western Cape, often found in citrus orchards, open grasslands and lawned gardens.
Notes: Seen busily probing the ground with the crest folded. The wings are large in relation to the general size and its flight has been likened to the jerky movements of a butterfly. Feeds on beetles, caterpillars, grubs, frogs and ant-lions. The call is a

musical 'hoop-hoop' but young birds make a sound resembling 'swee-sweet' when once they have left the nest. Breed from August to December, making a nest among stones, in a hole in the ground or in a bank. One nest is used repeatedly' about 5 eggs are laid, usually two or three times a year, and the nest is often very dirty and foul smelling. In Afrikaans: Hoephoep, in Sotho: Pupupu, in Zulu: u-Ziningweni, in Xhosa: u-Boye.

162. Acacia Pied Barbet *Lybius leucomelas* 18 cm R432

Field Identification: In adult birds the forehead and crown are red, with a yellow eyebrow above the eyes which ends in a white streak along the side of the head. There is a broad whitish streak running from the side of the bill down the side of the head, the rest of the head being black. Under the thick black bill the chin is black, with a pointed bib effect reaching down over the throat. Mantle and wing coverts are black spotted with lemon yellow and lightly streaked with offwhite, blackish wing plumage edged with offwhite. The rump is mainly lemon yellow streaked with black and tail feathers are blackish brown edged with pale yellow, underparts offwhite lightly streaked with black on flanks. Legs black, eyes dark brown. Females are the same and immature birds have no red on the forehead, the eyebrow is more greenish, and they are streaked below.
Distribution: Resident, and the only barbet present, in the south western Cape. Especially prevalent in the more northerly and easterly sections. Uncommon on the Cape Flats but increasing in the vicinity of Cape Town.
Notes: Usually seen alone or in pairs sitting on the tops of trees. Characteristically

restless, moving from one tree to another, flying directly and at considerable speed. Feeds on insects or fruit. Rather noisy birds with a loud nasal call – an almost trumpet-like 'tnar-tnar'. The courting call is rather like the call of the Hoopoe – a slurred 'poop-poop'. Uses dead tree trunks in which to excavate nests, or when not available, will use the nests of swallows. In Afrikaans: Bont Houtkapper, in Sotho: se-Rokolo.

163. Greater Honeyguide *Indicator indicator* 20 cm R440

Field Identification: The adult male has upper parts a sooty brown with a distinct white earpatch and a yellow streak on the shoulder. The wing coverts and rump are streaked with white, and there are three outer tail feathers which are a dirty white, central feathers dusky brown. The throat is sooty brown ending in a straight line around the neck; chest, belly and underparts offwhite. The eyes are brown, bill pinkish white, legs bluish green to grey. Adult females are a uniform sooty brown with no white earpatch or yellow shoulder streak, throat and underparts offwhite, beak black. Young birds are tinged with yellow, especially on the throat, and resemble the female in having a black bill.

Distribution: Rare but resident in the south western Cape, especially in pine and gum plantations. Only very few present in the more northerly areas.

Notes: Will guide men or animals to bees' nests by flying in short distances from tree to tree and calling repeatedly until the nest is reached, at which time it will either become silent or change the sound of the call. This species feeds on beeswax, larvae of insects, and a variety of insect species. A particularly tough skin seem to render them impervious to bee stings. Like cuckoos they are parasitic and most, or all, of the host's eggs, usually barbets, woodpeckers and bee-eaters, are broken by the female. It is believed that the chicks eject the host's young from the nest but it is more likely that the dead nestlings are got rid of by the parent birds after these nestlings have been attacked and killed by the newly hatched Greater Honeyguide, which is equipped with a wicked hook on the tip of the upper and lower mandible. These hooks gradually disappear as the chick develops and are entirely absent by the time it is ready to leave the host's nest. the sexes live separately but the male puts on a spectacular display of upward and downward swoops to attract the female to a mating site during the breeding season, which is from September to January. The call, which sounds like 'whit-purr-whit-purr' is repeated from seven to eleven times every minute. When guiding to a bees' nest the call is a continuous 'cha-cha-cha'. In Afrikaans: Groot Heuning-wyser, in Zulu: i-Ngede, in Xhosa: in-Takobusi, in Sotho: Tsese.

164. Ground Woodpecker *Geocolaptes olivaceus* 27 cm R445

Field Identification: The only woodpecker with a pinkish red belly. The head is brownish grey, the eyes offwhite, tinged with pink, the rump bright red. Upper parts are olivy brown sparsely spotted with white, tail plumage slightly darker barred with yellowish white. Throat and upper chest offwhite, bill and legs black. Females are similar and young birds are duller, having lower parts mottled with white and olive.

Distribution: Resident and fairly common in fynbos, on boulder-strewn hillsides and the lower mountain slopes, but not present in open flat country.

Notes: An unusual bird that has forsaken a normal life in trees for life on the ground. Its flight is rather heavy and when in flight the red rump becomes conspicuous. Hops along on the ground and is commonly seen in small parties, sitting very erect on rocky outcrops. This species has a sticky substance on the tongue used to trap insects. Feeds on ants as well as a variety of insects. The call resembles the screech made when a saw is sharpened with a file. Another call is 'chick-scream-chick-scream-chick'. Breeds from August to September when three to five white eggs are laid at the end of a long burrow, about a metre deep in a bank. In Afrikaans: Grond-spegt, in Xhosa: um-Nquangqandola, in Sotho: Uapaleome.

165. Cardinal Woodpecker *Dendropicos fuscescens* 15 cm R450

Field Identification: The adult male has forehead black and crown to nape crested in bright red. The rest of the head is silvery white streaked with black, with black nape and black moustache marks. Throat, belly and underparts are silvery white heavily streaked with black, tail black, barred with white and washed with golden. Upper parts are black barred with white and spotted on the wing shoulder. Bill black, legs greyish black, eyes brownish black. The female is similar, as can be seen from the photographs, but has the crown black. Immature birds resemble the male but are duller, with crown red and nape black.

Distribution: Widely distributed throughout the area but rare, nevertheless resident in woodland and indigenous bush, not in true forests.

Notes: Usually lands in the lower section of a tree, works its way

upwards to the higher branches and then flies off to the next tree. Drumming is rapid and not as noisy as in other larger species. Pairs will join other bird parties. Feed on insects in trees, mealie stalks, reeds and euphorbias. A quiet chittering is uttered by both sexes but the alarm call is a higher pitched shrill scream and when aggressive the cry is 'creek, creek, creek'. September and October are the months in which the Cardinal Woodpecker breeds in the Cape. Both sexes take a part in boring holes into dead tree trunks or into the branches of trees, the process taking about two weeks. Two or three white eggs are laid, incubation being by both sexes. The male often feeds the female on the nest. In Afrikaans: Kardinaal-spegt, in Zulu: i-Nqonqonda, in Xhosa: isi-Quola.

♀

166. Olive Woodpecker *Mesopicos griseocephalus* 20 cm R452

Field Identification: Differs from other woodpeckers in that it is neither spotted or barred. The adult male, photographed here, has a grey head with a red crested crown. Generally olivy green in colour with a yellow wash and a more brilliant yellow on the upper chest and wing shoulder, with underparts offwhite lightly streaked with olivy yellow and grey. The wings are edged with black and the black tail feathers are red at the base, with rump red. Eyes dark brown, bill a slaty grey, lighter below, legs grey. The female lacks any red on the head, having crown and throat grey but may have a little red at the nape. Immature birds are duller.

Distribution: Resident in forests, occurring mainly along the southern and eastern coastline towards Natal.

Notes: Will execute four or five strokes per second when drilling trees. Similar in habits to other species of woodpeckers but prefers small trees and small branches in large trees. Characteristically shakes its head from side to side when uttering its call which is a loud 'wer-chick' or Chir-r-r-re'. Feeds on insects. Breeds during October and November laying three white eggs. Both sexes assist in incubation. In Afrikaans: Gryskop-spegt, in Zulu: isi-qupamuti.

167. Thickbilled Lark *Galerida magnirostris* 18 cm R463

Field Identification: Adults are heavily built, dusky brown, with plumage edges offwhite, sides of face plain beige, tail plain dark brown and fairly square in flight.

Stout horn coloured bill, eyes brown, legs light brown. Young birds are mottled. The photograph shows the long hind-claw.

Distribution: Favours cultivated land and is the commonest lark in the wheatlands. Resident, occurring in pairs or small parties.

Notes: The male sings while rising into the air during the breeding season. Thickbilled Larks imitate other birds, but usually have a persistent double call note described as 'teee-wheatleooo'. Breeding time is from August to November and the nest, found near some plant on the ground, is a shallow hollow constructed from roots and grasses, containing two or three white or cream eggs, blotched in yellowish brown. In Afrikaans: Dikbeklewerik.

168. Spikeheeled Lark *Chersomanes albofasciata* 15 cm R474

Field Identification: Russet brown, streaked with black on crown, nape, mantle and back. Dusky brown flight feathers, tail feathers brownish, throat offwhite, underparts brownish slightly streaked with dusky. Eyes brown, bill slightly curved and fairly thin and pointed, greyish black. Legs and feet grey. The illustration clearly shows the extended hind claw. The female is smaller than the male and usually lighter in colouring, young birds are mottled, and nestlings, as seen here in the nest, are spotted with white above and greyish below.

Distribution: Prefers stony ground with little or low vegetation and the nest shown here is built in such a situation. Common in the Karoo along the lower Olifants River. Also reported in Riviersonderend and Langebaan.

Notes: Found in parties of six or eight, scurrying around the ground in mouselike movements. If chased will show considerable excitement before alighting and standing in a very upright manner in order to better watch the intruder. The voice is usually heard in flight and varies – a short 'chree-chree', a softer 'ploo-ploo-ploo' and also a rapid 'chitt-chitt-chitt-chew-chew-chew'. Feeds on beetles. The breeding

period is August to December. The nest is a deep cup made from dried rootlets and grass and will be placed under a plant or tuft of grass, usually facing south or east. Eggs number two or three and are pale green, mixed with yellow-brown, sepia and grey, spotted all over with brown spots concentrated at the thicker end in a ring. In Afrikaans: Vlakvoël, in Xhosa: u-Ngqembe, in Sotho: Motinyane.

169. Longbilled Lark *Certhilauda curvirostris* 20 cm R475

Field Identification: Upper parts russet brown with darker streaks and with plumage narrowly edged with offwhite. There is a prominent light eye-stripe and the lark tail is also narrowly edged with offwhite. Buff below streaked with blackish; chin and throat offwhite. The long brown bill is slightly downward-curved, eyes dark brown, legs yellowish. Females are similar and young birds appear mottled due to feather tips being lighter.

Distribution: A regular resident in indigenous bush, except the Fynbos, and partial to stony ground. Present throughout the area.

Notes: Stalks small insects and feeds on seeds as well. When eating assumes a crouching position as shown by the Longbilled Lark half hidden in the vegetation, but when looking around stands with an upright stance illustrated by the lark with his head raised. The usual call is 'churr-wee-wrr', young birds utter a 'chrrr'. The breeding season is from September to November and during this time display flights are evident, which take the form of an almost vertical rise from the ground, and then

146

a violent plummeting down while uttering a loud drawn out 'phee-yeeoo'. Two or three pale pink eggs, marked with yellowy brown or grey will be found in a nest of rough grass, placed under a tuft of grass or next to a stone. In Afrikaans: Langbek-lewerik.

170. Greybacked Finchlark *Eremopterix verticalis* 13 cm R485

Field Identification: The adult male, seen here on the nest, is russet brown with a white patch on the crown and on either side of the head, a white band across the hind neck and white patches on either side of the upper chest. The light edges to all the upper plumage gives a greyish appearance, underparts brown. The female is lighter and lacks the white patches. The stout finch-like bill is bluish grey, eyes brown, legs either brownish or bluish white. Young birds are grey, tipped with buff.

Distribution: Found north of Bellville but uncommon south of Malmesbury and east of the Hottentots Holland mountains. A common, restless species, with a preference for bare or newly ploughed land. Favours wheatlands and adjoining veld.

Notes: Occasionally found in fair-sized flocks but more usually in quite small parties. Look remarkably like finches on the ground but can be distinguished by the fact that they run instead of hop. When frightened they will fly off for a short distance and then fall to the ground again, or more rarely settle on a low bush. The call is a fairly sharp 'cheep' when rising from the ground, or a soft chirp while running around on the ground feeding. Breed December and January, the nest being a cup-shaped grass structure strengthened with other materials such as earth and stones. It is found under a small bush or tuft of grass. Eggs number two, white in colour, spotted with yellowy brown and grey. In Afrikaans: Grysrug-kaffertjie.

171. Redcapped Lark *Calandrella cinerea* 15 cm R488

Field Identification: Distinguishing features are the chestnut crested crown, not very prominent in this particular bird, and the chestnut patches on either side of the breast. Upper parts are light brown, with upper tail coverts chestnut and wing and tail feathers darker brown with outer web of outermost tail feathers white. There is a white eyebrow stripe, and chin, breast, belly and underparts are white. The female is similar and young birds look very speckled with darker plumage above edged with white. Eyes hazel, bill black, legs brown.

Distribution: Favour treeless arid areas, stubble lands and open thinly covered ground. Fairly widely distributed in the south western Cape.

Notes: Ground dwelling and resident, capable of running very fast over open ground uttering a 'cheep' or a 'tsheerk'. Also utters a short 'chick' in flight and will mimic the calls of other birds. The male utters a short musical phrase while hovering and diving high in the air. When surprised on the ground will fly off very low, drop suddenly and run off again immediately on alighting. Lives on the seeds of wheat and grasses. Breeding season is from August to December in the area. There are usually two creamy coloured eggs, with a fine freckling of sepia and grey, found in a cup-shaped nest formed from grasses. Occasionally the number varies up to four. In Afrikaans: Rooikop-lewerik, in Xhosa: in-Tubane or in-Tutyane.

172. European Swallow *Hirundo rustica* 18 cm R493

Field Identification: A distinguishing feature is the chestnut throat bordered with a bib-like broad band of black and a small amount of chestnut above the black bill. Upper parts are glossy blue-black, clearly illustrated in the photograph, and under-parts white. In flight the outermost tail-feathers are seen to be very elongated and all the tail feathers have a white mark on the underside forming a band across the tail. The eyes are brown, bill and legs black. The female has slightly shorter tail feathers and young birds are browner above, slightly mottled with white, the chestnut throat is paler, and tail feathers less elongated.

Distribution: Abundant in the summer months, being a common non-breeding migrant from the Palaearctic arriving in August and more especially in November. There have been a few records of them remaining until May, June and even July, but are gone by April. Very prevalent near water and cultivation and may be seen all over the Cape in flocks of hundreds, or even thousands, when roosting in reed beds.

Notes: They are often seen resting in large groups on telephone wires, and they gather in large numbers before migrating back to Europe at the start of the Cape winter. Birds ringed in South Africa have been recovered from Ireland in the west to Siberia in the east. The fastest recorded flight is that of a bird ringed in Johannesburg recovered 12,000 kilometres away in 34 days. Live on a variety of insects especially flying termites and are frequently seen flying low over grass stalks and pecking off insects. They breed at their northern breeding sites and often are almost ready to leave before gaining their full plumage with elongated tail feathers. Their usual call is a twittering 'tswit-tswit-tswit' and a warbling song heard on the wing just before their northern migration. In Afrikaans: Europese Swael, in Xhosa: u-Fabele, in Sotho: le-Fokotsane, in Zulu: i-Nkonyane.

173. Whitethroated Swallow *Hirundo albigularis* 17 cm R495

Field Identification: The white throat and sides of neck, and offwhite underparts, divided by a broad blue-black band, sometimes broken in the centre, which runs across the upper chest, distinguish this swallow. The chestnut forehead is more con-

spicuous than in the European Swallow but in flight the greyish wings and the white band on the underside of the tail are very similar, although the elongated outer tail feathers would help in identification. Eyes dark brown, bill black, legs greyish black. Female similar, young birds duller with chestnut patch on forehead lighter and smaller.

Distribution: A common summer migrant particularly to the lowlands and valleys of the south western Cape in areas near water. Generally arrives during August and leaves in April, breeding up until March with a peak in October. Nest sites are often found at culverts and low bridges.

Notes: Fly very fast and the slightly bent outline of the wings gives the appearance of large shoulders. Will be found in the areas already described as well as in urban areas, and the nest sites are returned to year after year. The nest is made from pieces of mud shaped into a half bowl and lined with soft feathers. Often it is under a bridge and young birds quite often fall out of the nests into the water beneath and are able to swim for short distances. Eggs usually number three and are white speckled with reddish brown and slate-blue, with these markings more concentrated at the larger end. Whitethroated Swallows live on insects and their call is a gentle twittering. In Afrikaans: Witkeel-swael.

174. Pearlbreasted Swallow *Hirundo dimidiata* 14 cm R498

Field Identification: This swallow is smaller than the Whitethroated Swallow, the tail is all black, clearly seen in the illustration, and lacks the white band present in other swallows. There is no chestnut colouring on the head and no dark chest band. Upper parts are a glossy blue-black, throat and underparts pearly white. The tail is

forked but the outer feathers are only slightly elongated; eyes brown, bill and legs black.

Distribution: A common, breeding, summer migrant to the valleys and lowlands of the south western Cape, building nests in buildings rather than under bridges. The delightful photograph shows the adult bird feeding her nestlings in such a nest.

Notes: Arrives early September leaving again by the beginning of March. The nests are constructed of pellets of mud formed into a half-bowl, lined with rootlets. This species live on insects and their flight pattern is similar to that of the European Swallow. Eggs number three or four and are snow white. In Afrikaans: Pêrelbors-swaeltjie.

175. Greater Striped Swallow *Hirundo cucullata* 20 cm R502

Field Identification: Both the Lesser and Greater Striped Swallows are distinguished from other swallows by striped underparts, but this species does not have such strongly marked stripes as the smaller variety. This particular bird appears to be posing for the camera in order to show his distinguishing features to advantage. The forehead, crown, nape and rump are reddish chestnut, with the mantle and upper wing plumage glossy blue black, the forward wing edge tinted with greyish pink. The ear-coverts are offwhite, underparts palest fawn lightly striped with narrow black stripes. The dark tail is deeply forked and banded with white on the underside. The female is similar and young birds have a duller colouring. Eyes brown, legs greyish brown, bill black.

Distribution: A very prolific summer migrant breeding in the area; found almost everywhere within easy reach of water, also in close association with human habitation.

Notes: Usually found in pairs but flocks of twenty or thirty may be observed when they arrive and after breeding. They will return year after year to the same nesting sites, usually in some building overhang, or less often in culverts or under bridges. The nest, with its long tubular entrance is formed from mud and lined with feathers and rootlets. The glossy white eggs number two to four. Food is derived from insects and the call is a pleasant twittering 'chissick'. In Afrikaans: Groot Streepswael, or Groot-streepborsswawel.

176. Lesser Striped Swallow *Hirundo abyssinica* 16 cm R503

Field Identification: Smaller in size than the previous species, the head and rump being a uniform brighter chestnut, but this fades before moulting, after the breeding season. Chin, throat, chest and underparts silky white heavily and broadly streaked with black – in fact from a distance this area can look very dark. Flight feathers are dusky, with mantle, scapulars and wing-coverts deep glossy blue-black. Tail feathers are dusky spotted with white and deeply forked. Eyes dark brown, bill and legs black. The female is similar and immature birds are mottled on the breast and generally paler and duller.

Distribution: A rare straggler from further east, where it is a summer migrant.

Notes: The flight pattern is slow, often gliding, and the call either 'tee-tee-tee' or 'turr-turr-turr', is often heard on the wing. Lives on beetles to a large degree but eats other insects as well. Occurs in small parties or in pairs building nests under an overhang next to a building, a bridge or a cliff, or where these are not found against a tree trunk. The nest is formed from mud pellets and will have a long unlined entrance tunnel and a cup lined with feathers containing two to four white eggs. In Afrikaans: Klein Streepswael.

177. African Rock Martin *Hirundo fuligula* 15 cm R506

Field Identification: Upper parts are sooty brown, chin and neck pale russet with lower parts sooty brown. The short tail is square and when in flight white spots placed in a band are evident. The eyes and legs are brown, bill black. The female is similar and young birds have similar colouring with feather tips russet.

Distribution: A common resident species breeding where there are rock-faces, cliffs, or, more usually on buildings.

Notes: The flight pattern is rather slow and there are frequent twists and turns with the result that the short squarish tail is fanned out showing the white spots. Often associate in flocks with other species of martins, swallow and swifts, usually being more active in the early morning or at dusk. The call is a high-pitched 'cheep-cheep-churr' repeated several times on the wing. A further call sounds like a soft twittering song. Feeds on insects. Nests built of mud pellets, like the one shown in the photograph, are usually found under the eaves or overhang of a building. Three or four white eggs, evenly speckled with brown and slate will be found inside, lying on a lining of feathers and bits of roots. In Afrikaans: Kransswael, on Xhosa: u-Nongu-bendala, in Sotho: le-Kabelane.

178. Brownthroated Sand Martin
Riparia paludocola 12 cm R509

Field Identification: Chin and throat a pale mousy brown with belly and underparts silvery white, although occasionally individual birds are brown below as well. All the upper parts, including the wings and tail are mousy brown. The shortish tail has

no spots and is only slightly forked, each side being fairly rounded, as can be seen in the photograph. Eyes are brown, legs and bill black. Sexes are the same and young birds have a more mottled appearance due to having buff tips to feathers.

Distribution: Widely distributed throughout the area and common wherever there is water.

Notes: A summer breeding migrant, frequenting rivers and streams where flocks hawk insects and nests are made in sandbanks. During the non-breeding season large flocks will be found roosting in reed beds. Nests may be quite separate or in the midst of colonies of birds numbering up to five hundred. To form a nest a burrow is excavated between forty five and sixty cms into a bank, the eggs are laid before the lining is added. Eggs, usually numbering two, but less often three to four, are snow white. The call is thin and reedy like a feeble 'svee-svee'. In Afrikaans: Afrikaanse Oewerswael, in Sotho: le-Kavelane.

179. Banded Sand Martin *Riparia cincta* 17 cm R510

Field Identification: A distinct white line over the dark hazel eye down to the small black bill, shown clearly in the photograph, is distinctive, as is the short square tail. The upper parts, including the wings and tail are mousy brown with the lower parts white, banded with a bib-shaped marking in mousy brown around the upper breast. The bill and feet are black. The female is similar and young birds have the feathers on the upper parts tipped with rust.

Distribution: A breeding summer migrant, of fairly large size, distributed throughout the area but not common.

Notes: The flight is slow and de-

liberate with many rests taken en route, typically on long grass stems or on wire fences. Feeds on insects found on grass tops, and is often found in open grassy country. Arrives towards the end of August and leaves again during April, during which time it will be found either alone or in pairs. The call is a fairly loud chattering 'chuk'. It is thought that old Kingfisher holes may be used as nests, anyway they are isolated, generally burrowed by the parent birds, and are about 80 cm deep in a sandbank. They have been recorded breeding in company with Pied Starlings. Three or four pure white eggs will be found on a pad of grass or roots at the end of the burrow. In Afrikaans: Gebande Oewerswael.

180. Black Sawwing *Psalidoprocne holomelas* 15 cm R511

Field Identification: An extremely rare picture of a Black Sawwing outside its burrow as this species usually enters and vanishes from sight immediately. A totally black swallow of slender build with a deeply forked slender tail and wings that cross over when closed as seen in the picture. The under-wing coverts are dark ashy brown and the black has an almost greenish iridescence. The female has a less forked tail and young birds lack the gloss. The eyes are dark brown, bill black, legs purplish black.

Distribution: Resident and found in the forested areas of the south western Cape, especially where large dark trees overhang water. Not common but fairly widely distributed.

Notes: Fly chiefly towards evening and are seen usually singly or in pairs. The flight is very fast and gracefully executed, flitting between the branches of the trees while hunting insects. They do not often utter a sound but sometimes, when alarmed, one will hear a soft chirp. Thought to rest in the foliage during the heat of the day. During the breeding season a burrow is dug in a sandbank sloping upwards for about 45 cms. The nest is padded with grass, pine needles and moss. One to three white eggs are laid. In Afrikaans: Saagvlerk-swael.

155

181. Black Cuckooshrike *Campephage flava* 22 cm R513

♀

Field Identification: The Black Cuckooshrike, adult male, is black with a dark blue gloss, and may have a bright yellow patch on the shoulder, while in other birds this is absent. The tail is fairly long and distinctly rounded, and there is a swollen bright yellow-orange gape, clearly evident in the photograph. The legs and bill are black, eyes dark brown. Females and young birds look entirely different with honey brown and whitish colouring above, barred with black on mantle, rump and tail coverts. The tail is brownish with bright yellow outer feathers. Throat and underparts white, with black bars, and sometimes a yellowish wash. Young birds have darker throats, more barring underneath and pointed tails.

Distribution: A rare species found in thick woodland which has been recorded in Somerset West, Stellenbosch, Kirstenbosch and Swellendam. Also found in lowland scrub along the coast.

Notes: The rarity of this species is sometimes questioned as it is a fairly silent bird and could quite easily be overlooked as it is usually hidden in thick foliage, quietly perching on a branch or creeping about in dense undergrowth. Seen flying from one patch of bush to another with a very distinctive flapping action. Feeds on insects off leaves, or from the ground, its food being derived from a fairly wide variety, as well as caterpillars and fruit. Although generally quiet, a low insect-like trilling note is sometimes uttered like 'wheeo-wheeo-eee-ee-e'. The nest, as seen in the photographs, will be in the fork of a tree and camouflaged with lichens. The breeding season is from October to December with the eggs numbering two or three and of a shiny bluish green speckled with olive brown and purple grey. In Afrikaans: Swart Katakoeroe, in Xhosa: u-Sasa.

182. Golden Oriole *Oriolus oriolus* 24 cm R519

Field Identification: The adult male is golden yellow from forehead to rump above, and from chin to underparts below. A heavy black stripe runs from the bill to the eye, with only a faint streak behind the eye, wings are black with some fine edges yellow, the tail black tipped with yellow. Eyes dark reddish, bill pinkish horn, legs dark grey. The female, shown at the nest with her four chicks in the photograph taken in Europe, is whitish on throat and chest with dark streaks, and the wing shoulder is tinged with brown. Immature birds are less yellow than the female below, and are more greenish yellow on crown and mantle.

Distribution: An uncommon, non-breeding migrant from the Palaearctic arriving during October, in the early spring, and leaving again in March. Favours dry woodlands with high trees. Seen at Somerset West every summer since 1955 and every year in fig trees at Klawervlei. Also sighted at Schrywershoek in Claremont, at Durbanville and Onrust, at Helderberg and Muizenberg.

Notes: Seen in small parties flying about in the tops of tall trees many still having the immature plumage of young birds. They live on a variety of insects and fruit and the call is a clear strong 'weela-weeeo' or if alarmed a harsh 'chrrr'. In Afrikaans: Europese Wielewaal.

183. Pied Crow *Corvus albus* 49 cm R522

Field Identification: A common species abundant throughout the area. All glossy black except for a broad white collar, and white on lower chest and belly. There are long black bristles around the curved black beak and the black plumage from chin to lower neck is rather full and bushy. Eyes brown, legs black and feathered half way. Females are the same and young birds are a duller black.

Distribution: Widely and commonly distributed throughout the area especially on the flats around Cape Town.

Notes: Where there is abundant food they appear in small parties but more usually they are seen in pairs. Will feed on animals or birds run over on roads, and will often feed at refuse dumps. They have been known to follow trains for scraps in some areas. Soar at a considerable height, repeating a raucous 'kwahk-kwahk'. Nest in tall trees or on telegraph poles. The breeding season is from September to October with eggs usually numbering four, but occasionally any number from one to seven. They are pale green, blotched with olive, violet-grey and brown. In Afrikaans: Witborskraai, in Sotho: Lokhokuba, in Xhosa: Gwahube, in Zulu: i-Gwabayi.

184. Black Crow *Corvus capensis* 50 cm R523

Field Identification: A plain black crow with a fairly slender black bill and black legs. The eyes are dark brown, females are similar and young birds are duller with a brownish wash on the head and chest.

Distribution: Occurs in localised areas and in those areas is common. Prevalent in the Darling and Bredasdorp districts. Prefers open country such as grainlands and

158

the Karoo, replacing the Pied Crow in some areas and being replaced by the White-necked Raven in more mountainous regions.

Notes: The rather narrow black bill is a distinguishing feature even in flight. Flocks occur numbering up to fifty birds, composed of immature and unmated birds; mated pairs are inclined to remain in fairly restricted areas. Not at all popular with grain farmers as they do considerable damage to crops. Apart from grain they feed on berries and fruit, carrion, frogs and insects. The breeding time is mainly from August to December, but could be any time between July and March. The nest, often seen on a telegraph pole as well as in an aloe or high up in a tree, is made from a platform of sticks, lined with any available feathers, bits of hair, string or wool, or even dung. Eggs number one to six, pink with small blotches of darker pink, grey and reddish-brown. Black Crows are noisy birds uttering a high-pitched 'kah' and a bubbling alarm note. The Afrikaans name is Swart Kraai, in Sotho: le-Khoa, in Zulu: i-Gwaba-bane, in Xhosa: i-Dakatye.

185. Whitenecked Raven *Corvus albicollis* 52 cm R524

Field Identification: The most distinguishing feature is the broad white collar around the hind neck. The rest of the bird appears a glossy black, but on closer inspection it is seen that the head and neck have a brownish wash over the black. There is a deep heavy curved beak with a white tip which distinguishes it from the Black Crow when in flight, and the collar is hidden from view. Females are similar but have a smaller bill and immature birds have the white collar marked with a certain amount of black.

Distribution: Widely distributed throughout the area and resident. Fairly common near rocky precipii or foraging over surrounding country. Often seen over the beaches of False Bay.

Notes: Regarded as a pest, as they plunder chicken and their eggs, small lambs and sick sheep. Often arrive at a carcass before the vultures and are seen feeding on small animals killed on roadways. A wary species well able to take care of them-

159

selves. Feed on any animal food as well as fruit. Known by two calls, one a deep-throated 'kraak', and the other a high-pitched nasal tone. The breeding season is from July to November, especially in September, and the nest will be found high up

in mountainous area, containing one to six eggs, pale green heavily streaked with olive, grey and brown. In Afrikaans: Withals-kraai, in Zulu: i-Gwababa, in Sotho: Lekhoaba, in Xhosa: i-Hwababa.

186. Southern Grey Tit *Parus afer* 15 cm R525

Field Identification: A fairly small plump little bird with head, nape, throat and centre belly black. A distinct broad white stripe runs from the gape, under the eye, and curves downwards to the sides of the belly. There is a whitish patch below the nape merging with the back and wing colouring, which is very finely striped in white, black and olive, giving a lightish olive appearance. The flight feathers are dusky, the rounded tail black, finely edged with offwhite, underparts ashy beige. The eyes are dark brown, the short stout bill black, and the legs lead grey. Females are similar and young birds have flight feathers edged with beige, upper parts more brownish.

Distribution: Resident in the Strandveld in well grown indigenous bush, but not present along the southernmost and eastern coastline.

Notes: A noisy species often found in mixed parties of birds, busily foraging for insects and caterpillars – the picture shows one that did not get away. Favours rather dry bushy terrain and has a variety of ringing calls – 'peet-choe-choe', 'titsikrur-krur-krur', give-ear-give-ear' and 'twit-twit-twit'. Breeds from August to October, making a nest in a hole in a bank, a tree, or even a fence pole. The nest will be warmly lined with some soft material and will contain three to four white eggs, colourfully speckled with violet, red and grey. In Afrikaans: Piettjoutjou, in Sotho: Sekhekha.

187. Cape Rockjumper *Chaetops frenatus* 23 cms R540

Field Identification: The adult male is a beautiful glossy black and reddish chestnut bird with touches of white and a brilliant red eye. Upper parts and tail black, with reddish chestnut rump. There is a white streak from the base of the black bill down the sides of the neck, a suggestion of a white streak over the eye, a white patch and a few light streaks on the black wings, and the outer tail feathers are tipped with white. The lower chest and belly is vivid reddish chestnut. The female is duller with dark ash-grey on head, neck and upper parts, and no pure white streaks as with the male bird. The underparts are reddish chestnut often sparsely streaked with black. Legs and feet black. The plumage of this species is fairly full and fluffy.

Distribution: Favours boulder-strewn mountain slopes that are south facing in the south western Cape.

Notes: Seen in pairs or small parties, jumping from rock to rock, or running along the ground between boulders, rarely using their short rounded wings. Feed on in-

sects, which are found by digging in soil or dead leaves, and flicking the loose debris sideways with their bills. Grasshoppers and gekkos form part of their diet. Shy and wary, they are often identified more by their call – a rapidly descending 'pee-pee-pee' – than by actually being spotted. Eggs are laid in an untidy large cupshaped nest of dry grass, moss and lichens, hidden under stones and built by both the male and female. Breeding season is from September to November. The eggs normally number two and are pure white. In Afrikaans: Bergkatlagter.

188. Cape Bulbul *Pycnonotus capensis* 20 cm R543

Field Identification: A white wattle around the eye and a more uniform colouring of head and breast distinguish this species from the Redeyed Bulbul which is present further north. The general colouring is sooty brown on the crested head, back, wings, tail and underparts, with under tail-coverts bright yellow, eye and chin area blackish brown. The eyes, legs and bill are black. Females and young birds are similar but young birds lack the white wattle for the first three months. The tail feathers are fairly wide, the tip being straight and square.
Distribution: A widespread, common resident bird wherever there are fruit-bearing trees and bushes.

Notes: Very unpopular in orchards, where they do great damage to the fruit harvest, and abundant in the dense thickets of exotic wattles that have spread over the southern Cape. Lively noisy birds usually seen flying around in pairs, and keen visitors at feeding tables where they become quite tame. Feed on berries and fruit and become covered in pollen when feeding at flowers. The calls are cheerful liquid sounds like 'piet-majol' or 'piet-le-wiet' as well as a soft melodious song. Breeds from August to December, with a peak in September, and a few February to March records exist as well. The nest, shaped like a shallow open bowl, is well concealed in a bush and is made from twigs, roots and other vegetable matter. Eggs number two or three and are pinkish, with red and slate markings. In Afrikaans: Kaapse Tiptol.

189. Sombre Bulbul *Andropadus importunus* 21 cm R551

Field Identification: Often identified only by its call as it is noisy, but remains very still and well hidden in dense foliage. Its fairly drab colouring assists in camouflage. All the upper parts including the head, back tail and wings are a dull olivy gold, which blends easily with surrounding foliage; underparts are beige with a lemon wash. Eyes pale cream, bill black, legs dark grey. The sexes are the same and immature birds have a yellow ring around the eye and a horn-coloured bill.

Distribution: Inhabits dense indigenous forest areas of the south western Cape but is virtually absent from the Hottentots Holland, although recently there have been a few recordings. Favours tree-enclosed rivers and woodland of mixed exotics.

Notes: Has a rapid and direct flight pattern, characterised by very fast wingbeats. Food is derived from berries, fruits and certain insects. Utters a clear loud whistling 'willie' followed by a softer chuckling 'chuke-a-chuke-a-chuke', but in alarm there will be heard a quick repeated 'willie'. Also keeps up a short cheerful song heard most often during spring. Breeds from October to January, the nest being an ill-concealed thin base of roots and twigs, with two buff coloured eggs with marks of grey, green and brown. In Afrikaans: Willie, in Xhosa: i-Nkwili, in Zulu: i-Wili.

190. Olive Thrush *Turdus olivaceus* 24 cm R553

Field Identification: Entire head and back a dusky olivy grey with flight feathers and tail somewhat darker. The eyes are brown and a distinguishing feature is the yellow bill. The chin, throat and upper breast are whitish streaked with dusky brown, belly and lower flanks rufous chestnut, legs yellowish gold. Females are similar and young birds have upper parts with lighter streaks, underparts spotted with dusky. Two nestlings are seen in the nest.

Distribution: Found in densely treed areas throughout the south western Cape, and has fairly recently become an inhabitant of urban gardens.

Notes: Flies rapidly and during the courting season the male puffs himself up, spreads his tail and wings, and will circle the female on the ground. Usually seen scratching on the ground for worms and caterpillars, but if disturbed will fly rapidly to the nearest bush and hop along the branch in agitation; also feeds on fruits and seeds. Utters a quick 'tsit' when launching into flight, a lower 'tschuck-tschuck' when alarmed, and a short melodious range of notes 'wheety-wheety-wheety'. This species is an excellent mimic of surrounding noises. Breeds throughout the year with a peak in spring. Eggs usually number two or three, of a greenish-blue colour, dotted with slate grey and brown. The nest, illustrated in the photograph, is about three metres from the ground in the fork of a tree. In Afrikaans: Olyf Lyster, in Sotho: u-Muswi, in Xhosa: um-Swi.

191. Cape Rockthrush *Monticola rupestris* 21 cm R559

Field Identification: Adult male has head, neck and chin slate blue, chest chestnut fading to a lighter gold on underparts and under tail. Mantle and scapulars brown, flight feathers blackish brown, rump and upper tail plumage tawny chestnut, with two central tail feathers black. Eyes dark brown, bill and legs black. the female has head, neck and chin mousy brown, mantle and scapulars dark brown narrowly edged with small broken bars of brown, underparts and rump chestnut, tail rufous

164

♀

chestnut, with two central feathers blackish. Immature birds are heavily streaked below with brown and white, but in other respects resemble the female. Nestlings are spotted with buff and brown.

Distribution: Common in the mountainous areas and regular in fynbos.

Notes: Has a characteristic habit of flicking its wings after landing. Used to be considered as being only in mountainous areas, where it is still common, but today occurring right down to the seashore in the south western Cape. Has adapted to living near human habitation. Utters a loud clear whistling note like 'chireewoo-chirri-wee-roo' from its perch on the top of rocks, aloes, bushes or trees. The alarm call is a sharp 'charr'. Lives on insects, centipedes, small molluscs, frogs, seeds and berries. Builds a nest of loose bits and pieces of vegetation in a rocky crevice underneath an overhang, in which three to five pale blue eggs – sometimes spotted with rust – are laid. Breeding takes place from October to February. In Afrikaans: Kaapse Kliplyster, in Zulu: i-Kwelamatsheni.

192. Sentinel Rockthrush *Monticola explorator* 18 cm R560

Field Identification: This species is less common than the preceding Cape Rock-thrush, and although the colour differentiation between the male and female is similar, certain characteristics make the differences between the two species clear. The Sentinel Rockthrush is smaller, the male, seen in the photograph at the nest, has the grey-blue colouring extending to the back and upper chest, and the female has head, neck, throat and chest whitish streaked with brown. Wing and tail feathers are brownish black, with the remainder of the plumage tawny golden. Eyes and legs are dark brownish black, bill black. Young birds are barred and spotted with black and brown, similar to the young of the Cape Rockthrush, nestlings are seen in the photograph.
Distribution: Similar to that of the Cape Rockthrush, but has not adapted to human habitation and is considerably less common.

Notes: A very lively bird with a pronounced upright stance. Found on open hillsides feeding on ants and beetles, as well as berries and seeds. Has a clear whistling call but not as loud as the Cape Rockthrush. Breeding takes place from September to December when a rather small nest is formed in the crevice of a rock or sometimes on the ground, typically under a protective rocky overhang, so beautifully illustrated in the photograph. Three small round pale blue eggs are laid, which may be spotted with rust. In Afrikaans: Langtoon-kliplyster, in Xhosa: um-Ganto.

193. Mountain Chat *Oenanthe monticola* 19 cm R564

Field Identification: The adult male is variable in colour but always has the same pattern of white shoulder patch, rump and outer tail feathers. The remainder of the plumage may be black with a grey crown and nape, wholly black, or grey with black flight feathers. Belly and underparts are whitish, eyes dark brown, bill and legs black. The female is a sooty brown, except for the upper and under tail coverts and the outer tail feathers, which are white. Young birds resemble the female but young males have a certain amount of white on the shoulder. The female is seen with nestling in the nest built in the cleft of a rock.

Distribution: Resident in mountainous or hilly areas where there are plenty of rocks. Usually seen perched in pairs or small parties on a rocky promontory. Resident in many places, particularly in Mamre, Malanshoogte and Brandvlei North.

Notes: Has a characteristic flight pattern soaring off from its conspicuous perch for a short distance, dropping suddenly, and then flying at a lower level for another short distance. When alighting the Mountain Chat flicks its wings and jerks its tail. Attracted to garden feeding table and lives on young grasshoppers and other insects. Utters a clear ringing song, a cheerful whistle and a chattering alarm call. Breeding season is usually September to January, but could be a little extended before and after that period. The nest is usually found under stones on rocky hillsides, but other sites, in stone walls or in guttering have also been recorded. The nest is formed from grass and other vegetable matter, clumsily constructed in a bowl shape. Two or three greenish blue eggs, speckled with brownish pink, are laid. In Afrikaans: Bergwagter, in Sotho: Khaloti or le Tsoanafeki.

194. Capped Wheatear *Oenanthe pileata* 18 cm R568

Field Identification: The male and female are identical with white forehead and eyestripe above the eye, as well as a biblike white chin and throat. The crown, sides of head and broad band across the breast are black. Upper parts and flight feathers are russet brown, the flight feathers being edged with blackish, belly and underparts whitish, flanks chestnut. A distinctive feature in flight is the white rump and basal half of the outer tail feathers. The remainder of the tail is black. Eyes dark brown, bill and legs black. Young birds have no chest band and are mottled above with buff, and below with tawny brown.

Distribution: A fairly rare resident, or a partial migrant, in open places; but quite

numerous in the wheatlands of Malmesbury. Seen regularly in ploughed lands, grain fields and pastures, but not in large numbers.

Notes: A lively little bird, with an upright stance, that characteristically hops around with a great deal of jerking of wings and flicking of tail. Particularly noisy during the breeding season, which is from August to November, with a peak in September and October. Imitates other bird calls and even farmyard animals, but has a variety of pretty notes as well, and will continue singing them until dusk, giving this species the name 'Nagtegaal'. Food is derived from a variety of insects such as ants, flies, locusts, butterflies and caterpillars. Three to five pale greenish or bluish white eggs, lightly marked with pink speckles, are laid in a padded nest in a hole – often a rat burrow – in open ground. In Afrikaans: Skaapwagter, in Xhosa: is Xaxabesha or in-Kotyeni, in Sotho: Thoromeli.

195. Familiar Chat *Cercomela familiaris* 15 cm R570

Field Identification: A distinguishing feature is the central dark brown stripe extending the whole length of the tail, seen clearly when in flight. The tail when folded appears dark brown, as can be seen in the photograph. The rump and remaining tail feathers are gold and russet, with the tip of the entire tail banded with dark brown. Apart from the tail plumage it is quite difficult to distinguish this bird from the next species, the Sicklewinged Chat. Upper parts are tawny brown with rust coloured ear-coverts, underparts lighter tawny, wings dusky, eyes brown, bill and legs black. The female is the same and immature birds are darker and speckled. Nestlings are seen in the nest.

Distribution: A common chat resident in rocky areas.

Notes: Flicks its wings sideways and forwards, and flicks its tail as well. A lively, active species becoming quite tame around human habitations if unmolested. An interesting point is that this species used to eat grease from the old wagon wheels, and was given the name 'Spekvreter'. Pursues insects in flight, especially flies. Is fairly quiet but utters a low 'tjree-tjree-tjree' or an alarmed 'whee-chuck-chuck'. Breeds

from August to December with a peak in September and October. Will make a nest in a hole or under some overhang among rocks, as seen in the photograph, but near homesteads will use a hole in a wall, an old tin – or even a kettle has been recorded! The nest is a fairly deep cup roughly made of grass and rootlets, and then lined with softer material such as feathers, or hair and wool when available. Eggs usually number three and are greenish blue, speckled with brown. In Afrikaans: Spekvreter, in Sotho: le Tlerenyane or Phophorokhosa.

196. Sicklewinged Chat *Cercomela sinuata* 15 cm R572

Field Identification: There is a greater contrast between the upper and lower parts than with the Familiar Chat, the lower parts being lighter and the rump a more distinctly golden rufous. In flight there is no dark line down the centre of the tail but there is a broad blackish terminal band. Eyes brown, bill and legs black. Females are similar and young birds are spotted above and the lower plumage is edged with brown.

Distribution: Found in the drier areas and resident in indigenous bush and pastures; found also in ploughed land and grain fields.

Notes: Favours open ground with sparse vegetation and is seen flying from one low perch to another dropping down now and again to take insects. Flicks its wings a great deal. Breeding time is from September to January, when two to five eggs of a greenish blue tone, indistinctly marked with light rust, are laid in a neatly made cupshaped nest of grass and moss, lined with tendrils of soft vegetation. The nest is found on the ground at the base of a small bush or plant. In Afrikaans: Vlaktespekvreter.

197. Anteating Chat *Myrmecocichla formicivora* 18 cm R575

Field Identification: The adult male is smoky brown with a white shoulder mark, and the inner webs of half the flight feathers are white as well. Old female birds often develop white wing-coverts, but younger females are entirely brown. Young

birds are like the female but a redder brown. Eyes dark brown, bill and legs black. The very rapid wing beat and characteristic fluttering, when white 'windows' in the wings are seen, serve as a means of identification.

Distribution: First recorded in the south western Cape in 1955. In the intervening years it has extended its range and is now found as far south as Somerset West, with breeding records in the Hottentots Holland.

Notes: Usually seen in pairs perched with a very upright stance on an antheap, a low bush, or a fence pole. Will hover and drop down onto the perch and then rise up again in a bouncy manner and fly about with much fluttering of wings. Feeds on termites. Breeding takes place from October to January and the nest is sometimes burrowed in a bank, but more often it is in the upper part of an antbear burrow, and will be in a chamber at the end of the burrow, padded and lined with grass and rootlets. The eggs number three to four, usually pure white, but very occasionally lightly speckled with brown. The call is a raucous 'peek' and the male also sings a short song of clear whistled notes. In Afrikaans: Swartpiek, in Sotho: Thume, in Xhosa: isa-Nzwili.

198. Stonechat *Saxicola torquata* 14 cm R576

Field Identification: A handsome, plump, well known little bird, with head, nape, chin, throat, back, wings and tail black. There is a white patch on the sides of the neck, on the wings and the upper tail coverts. The chest and flanks are a bright chestnut and the lower belly offwhite. The female is tawny with black streaks in head, mantle and scapulars and white patches on wings, rump and upper tail coverts, all clearly seen in the photograph of the female at the nest. Young birds have upper and under parts speckled, nestlings are brownish as seen in the nest. Eyes, bill and legs black.

Distribution: A common resident in open country favouring treeless areas with low scrub, or moist flats along streams.

Notes: Usually seen in pairs, perched on a grass stem or low bush, from where it hops to the ground to secure the insects it feeds on. Will also catch dragonflies and flying termites in the air. A quiet bird, occasionally uttering a 'wheet-chak-chak' while flicking its tail and wings. Also sings a short bright song. Breeds from July to December and lays three or four pale green eggs, with reddish markings. The nest, as can be seen, is constructed of grass and lined with softer material. It

is usually concealed under a branch or in a clump of grass, reeds or other vegetation. In Afrikaans: Bontrokkie; in Xhosa: i-Ncape, in Zulu: is-Ncapela, in Sotho: Hlatsinyane.

199. Cape Robin *Cossypha caffra* 18 cm R581

Field Identification: The head, nape and wings are dark dusky grey with a slight olivy tinge. A long white stripe extends from the bill and over the eye. Chin is light golden, throat and upper chest rich deep chestnut, lower chest, belly and underparts slaty blue. The rump and tail are chestnut, the latter having a blackish stripe down the centre and tipped with dusky brown. Eyes brown, bill and legs black. The sexes are similar and young birds are plain brown lightly spotted.

Distribution: An abundant resident, common to open country and widely distributed, as well as being prevalent in gardens where shrubberies afford a retreat.

Notes: Found in pairs but venture into the open only where surrounding vegetation is near at hand in case of any alarm. Characterised by a jerky twitching of the chestnut tail. The diet is very varied and includes spiders, a variety of insects, worms, small frogs, lizards, berries and small soft fruits. The alarm call is a sharp 'wadeda' and the normal call sounds like 'Jan-Fred-erik'. Favours the bank of a stream thickly overgrown with ferns and other plants to build its nest, but it is sometimes found hidden in a hole, in a tin or even in old debris such as a disused flower pot. The nest is made of bits of twigs, loosely massed together with grass and leaves, but neatly lined with fine tendrils or rootlets. Breeding takes place in July, when two or three white eggs, with a greenish pink tinge, or sometimes speckled with pink or light brown, are laid. In Afrikaans: Janfrederik, in Xhosa: u-Gaga, in Zulu: u-Gaka, in Sotho: Mokhofe.

200. Karoo Scrub Robin *Erythropygia coryphaeus* 17 cm R583

Field Identification: A nondescript sandy brown bird slightly darker above than below, with a whitish throat and eyestripe above and below the eye, and white terminal tips to the outer black tail feathers. In flight the tail is fan-shaped. Young birds have back barred, with general mottling and white eye-stripe. Eyes brown, bill and legs blackish.

Distribution: A very common species of the drier sandy regions, resident in indigenous bush all over the area, but not in Macchia.

Notes: A lively little bird spending most of its time on the ground looking for insects. Feeds on berries as well. Will dance about excitedly flicking open its fan-shaped tail when disturbed, before darting to cover in the lower part of an adjoining bush. Fairly bold and inquisitive and will make a great fuss and noise if it sights a predator, such as a cat or a snake, the alarm call being a harsh grinding note. Also utters a short ringing call. The breeding season is from July to December, when a nest of dry grass,

rootlets and moss, lined with softer material, will be constructed on the ground, hidden in surrounding vegetation, as shown in the photograph. Eggs number two or three, and are a pale blue green with speckles of rust and streaks of purplish grey. In Afrikaans: Slangverklikker.

201. Cape Reed Warbler *Acrocephalus gracilirostris* 17 cm R604

Field Identification: Brownish rufous above with darker wing and tail plumage. Light eye stripe and sides of head light beige. Chin, throat and upper chest offwhite, underparts yellowish beige. Eyes hazel, bill brown with base pinkish buff, legs dark brown. Larger than the next species, the African Marsh Warbler, and more rufous than the following species, the African Sedge Warbler.

Distribution: Widely distributed and resident in reedbeds, from which it usually excludes the African Marsh Warbler. Seen in open reeds growing on the borders of lagoons, rivers, streams and permanent marshes.

Notes: Lives on insects taken from the reeds, but has been recorded as eating small frogs as well. Very inquisitive and attracted to anything unusual. Utters a short loud cheerful song, which is not just a repitition of a short phrase, but a burst of melodic notes arranged in a short but complete song. The nest, so beautifully shown in the photograph, is unmistakable, as it is a cone-shaped structure plaited around reed

stems, in the classical marsh-warbler style, and almost always placed over water. The cone has a deep cup and is lined with fine soft material. The breeding season is from September to December, when two or three white, or white tinged with green or blue, eggs, thickly covered with fine spots, varying in colour from black to brown to ash grey, are laid. In Afrikaans: Kaapse Rietsanger.

202. African Marsh Warbler
Acrocephalus baeticatus **12 cm R606**

Field Identification: Similar to the Cape Reed Warbler, but smaller, with no white eyebrow and lighter yellowish legs. Brownish above with darker wing and tail plumage, yellowish buff to offwhite below with white chin. Eyes brown, bill brown above with lower bill pinkish horn.

Distribution: Found in marshy areas and very frequently in reedbeds as well as in wattle scrub and in gardens. A common local migrant occurring as a summer breeding visitor.

Notes: A fairly tame bird often found in gardens yet tending to keep to fairly thick vegetation and revealing its presence by its warbling song uttered prior to nesting. The sounds are very varied, but there is an interspersed 'churr' and 'churra' occurring frequently. The nest is a small deep cup bound to a support like the reeds shown in the photograph. It is constructed from grass, reeds and leaves and lined with softer material. The breeding season is September to November in the Cape. Eggs number two or three and are round with brownish and grey marking on pale green or bluish white. In Afrikaans: Klein Rietsanger.

203. African Sedge Warbler
Bradypterus baboecala **16 cm R609**

Field Identification: All upper parts a darkish brown, with a pale beige eyestripe and underparts. The chin is offwhite and the throat streaked. The tail feathers are broader, longer and more rounded than the Cape Reed Warbler, the central tail feathers being twice as broad. Eyes brown, bill black with a lighter base, legs brownish.

Distribution: Widely distributed throughout the area and regular in permanent marshes. Seldom seen due to its skulking habits and desire to remain hidden.

Notes: Always found near water, usually creeping about in matted rushes and weeds. Displays a certain amount of inquisitiveness but even when investigating will do so from a concealed vantage point. The call sounds like that made when a stick is held to the spokes of a revolving wheel, 'tirr-tuk-tuk-tuk' or a series like 'crak-crak-crak', ending with a gurgling sound and a 'purring' of the wings. Breeding takes place from September to November when a nest is made, from dry rushes or weeds, into a rather untidy plaited cone supported in rushes, but not bound to the rushes as with the Cape Reed Warbler. Two pale cream eggs are laid, finely spotted with yellowish brown and a pale ashy colour. In Afrikaans: Kaapse Vleisanger.

204. Knysna Scrub Warbler *Bradypterus sylvaticus* 14 cm R611

Field Identification: Very similar to the African Sedge Warbler but with a slightly greyer tone to the overall brown. The tail seen fully extended is not as broad and is fairly short with a rounded tip. The wing and tail plumage is darker than the head and underparts and the chin is speckled beige, eyes dark brown, bill brownish, lighter below, legs pinkish olive brown. Immature birds have chin speckled white.
Distribution: Lives in bramble thickets in wooded kloofs, a rare bird thought to be found only on Table Mountain in this area, but so shy that its status is difficult to establish.
Notes: Lives in dense undergrowth on the damper south eastern slopes of Table Mountain and is to be found in bramble thickets. Utters a lovely song from deep in its hideaways. First of all one hears single high pitched notes sounded at intervals, then speeded up lower notes, until the sound develops into a bubbling trill. Breeding takes place in September and October and the nest, as seen in the photograph, is a large rounded shape made from dried vegetable matter, lined with softer material. It is to be found under the protection of a leafy canopy and well hidden in a thicket. There will be three pinky-white eggs, finely marked with tiny red spots. In Afrikaans: Knysna-ruigtesanger.

205. Victorin's Scrub Warbler *Bradypterus victorini* 16 cm R612

Field Identification: The male, seen in the first photograph, is rich brown above, including the tail feathers, which are not broad, and with a greyish tone to the head. Chin and throat are a golden cinnamon, breast, belly and underparts reddish brown, sparsely and lightly streaked with buff. Iris golden, bill greyish, paler below, legs

♀

brown. The female, in the second picture, illustrates the duller greyish brown above and duller cinnamon below, with more buff streaks than in the male bird. Nestlings are blackish above and greyish black below streaked with white.

Distribution: Common and resident in thick bush on Macchia covered hill slopes. Favours wet and misty mountain slopes where cover is thick, and is found in rocky kloofs and along mountain streams.

Notes: Once again this species is heard probably more often than it is seen, and if disturbed it scuttles through the undergrowth and could easily be mistaken for a mouse. Apart from this fact it has the ability to be an excellent ventriloquist, projecting its call to another area. The song has a varying number of phrases, going from low to high-pitched notes like 'twiddy-twee-twit, twiddy-twee-twit' gaining in speed and ending in four or five low notes. There is also an alarm call which is a loud 'purr'. September and October are the breeding months for this species and the nest is to be found among grassy vegetation but usually off the ground. It is constructed in three sections, first the roughly woven grass base, then a section of dead leaves and bark, and thirdly a deep cup of fine grass. Eggs number two and are pinkish-white dotted with red. In Afrikaans: Rooibors-ruigtesanger.

206. Grassbird *Sphenoeacus afer* 21 cm R618

Field Identification: Sometimes referred to as a lollipop bird as a distinctive feature is the long, full, pointed chestnut and brown plumage of the tail, which is generally kept tightly together like a stick, not as displayed in this unusual photograph. Fore-head, crown and sides of face are chestnut with sparse black streaks on the crown. Mantle, back and primary wing-coverts are black edged with buff, rump chestnut. Chin is greyish buff with a black moustache stripe down the side of the neck, under-parts greyish buff streaked with black. Eyes dark brownish red, bill black above, grey below, legs slate grey.
Distribution: Resident in long grass as shown in the photograph, widely distributed throughout the area.
Notes: Often seen sunning itself on a perch among long grass or weeds. At other times creeps around the ground surrounding the tufts of grass, and if disturbed, will fly awkwardly with its short rounded wings to another spot a short distance away. The call is a long sustained note like 'pee-ee-ee-ee', and when alarmed there is a high-pitched 'chee-chee-chee'. Breeding takes place most often in August but could be any time during the period from July to December. The nest is constructed in the centre of a tuft of grass, shown clearly in the photograph, with the bowl-shaped structure loosely woven from blades of grass. It will contain two or three pale grey or white eggs spotted with grey. In Afrikaans: Grasvoël, in Xhosa: itshitshi or u-dwetya.

207. Rufouseared Warbler *Malcorus Pectoralis* 15 cm R619

Field Identification: The rufous ear coverts, slightly lighter in the female, are the most obvious feature for identification. The centre of the head from bill to nape, hind neck, and upper parts, are streaked with black, white and beigy brown. Chin, throat and upper belly are white with a black band around the lower throat, underparts whitish, slightly streaked with blackish and rufous. Eyes reddish brown, bill black, legs pinkish flesh.

Distribution: Has been recorded from Table Mountain and its range appears to have contracted during the last one hundred years. Recorded from Mamre north, from Cape Town and Lion's Head and breeding on the Cape Flats. Inhabits dryish areas where vegetation is sparse.

Notes: The tail of the Rufouseared Warbler, hidden in the nest in the photograph, is long and thin and characteristically held upright. Seen in pairs or small parties darting quickly from one bush to another and then dropping out of sight to the ground. Most of its time is spent on the ground looking for insects. Calls vary from a loud continuous 'tee-tee-tee-tee' to a softer 'chit-it' or 'chrit'. Breeds from spring to early autumn, building a neat little oval nest of grass lined with feathers and silky seeds. It will be in a small bush and placed near the ground, containing between three and seven palest blue or white eggs. In Afrikaans: Rooioor-kleinjantjie.

208. Crombec *Sylvietta rufescens* 11 cm R621

Field Identification: A small bird distinguished by an extremely short tail and a fairly long curved dusky brown bill. The upper parts, including the tail and flight feathers, are greyish brown with the sides of face speckled buffish, underparts light yellowish buff, eyes brown, legs yellowish brown.

Distribution: Sparingly distributed in Macchia and wattle but common in the drier thornveld, open savanna and scrub areas. Prevalent in the Strandveld and other karoo type situations.

Notes: Has a rapid darting flight as it flies from one perch to another. Usually found in pairs or small family parties when searching for insects on the ground among twigs and leaves. Utters a shrill but pretty call 'peep-peep-peep' as well as two others 'richi-chichi-chichirr' and 'krrip-koop-kripkrip-kree'. Breeding in the south western Cape takes place from August to November, with a peak in September and October. A typical site for the nest would be suspended from the inside branches of a wattle or thorn tree. The nest so beautifully shown in the photograph is made from dry grass and fibres, shaped like an open purse, and lined with vegetable down. The outside is usually covered with spider webs. Eggs number two or three, white with greenish grey and brown markings. In Afrikaans: Stompstert, in Zulu: Ndibilitshe.

209. Barthroated Apalis *Apalis thoracica* 13 cm R622

Field Identification: A small round bird with upper parts, including the tail and the sides of face, grey, with a green wash on the back. The light yellow iris is in distinct contrast to the dark head and black lores and bill; the throat is white, banded below with a black half collar, underparts offwhite with a variable amount of pale yellow shading, legs pinkish. Females are duller in colouring.
Distribution: A common resident in the south western Cape, found in heavily treed kloofs, thick indigenous bush and along tree lined streams.
Notes: Creeps about among the trees and bushes looking for caterpillars and other insects and does not seem to be disturbed by the presence of onlookers. Tends to be inquisitive but is more often discerned by its loud whistling call than by being spotted in its thickly vegetated habitat. The call note 'pil-pil' or pilly-pilly' is often answered with a similar but softer call. Another call is a loud 'tic-tic-tic-tic' and a long drawn out 'chwee-chwee'. Breeding takes place from August to December and a favoured site for the nest is in creepers or overhanging vegetation on a bank, in sparsely-leafed bushes or in thick grass. It is carefully constructed in soft material and fine grass, lined with vegetable down and then festooned externally with moss and spider webs. This is well illustrated in the photograph. It is pear-shaped with an

entrance on the side, nearer to the top. Eggs number three or four and are pale greenish-blue or more rarely pinky-white with red-brown spots at the thicker end. In Afrikaans: Bandkeel-kleinjantjie, in Xhosa: u-Gxakweni, in Sotho: Setholemoru.

210. Fantailed Cisticola *Cisticola juncidis* 11 cm R629

Field Identification: Blackish brown above with feathers edged with buff. During the non-breeding season the light edging is wider and the bird looks lighter in colour. In breeding plumage the upper parts are brown streaked with blackish. The female is like the male in non-breeding plumage. The throat is white with underparts pale buff, except in the breeding male, when the underparts are more golden. The rump is rufous, the fan shaped tail dusky above, edged with offwhite, silvery white below; both above and below the tail has a sub-terminal spotted band of black narrowly edged with white. Eyes hazel, bill grey, legs pinky flesh. Immature birds are more rust coloured.

Distribution: Resident in short wet grassland and in lucern. First recorded in this area about 1930 but now a common breeding species.

Notes: Feeds on tiny insects and spends most of its time on the ground, not being seen often during the non-breeding season. If disturbed will make a short flight uttering an alarm call which is a shrill excited 'zit-zit-zit'. Breeding takes place during the summer months, from November to March, and at this time the male executes a display flight about 15 metres high in the sky uttering a call like 'klink' and dipping as each note, spaced a few second apart, is uttered. The nest is formed from drawing long growing grass together and binding it with strands of other vegetation into the shape of a bottle, with the opening at the top. These nests are extremely difficult to find. Three to five white or pale blue eggs, speckled with red and grey, are laid, and at that stage vegetable down is added to the inside of the nest until it is very well padded, by which time the eggs are hatched. In Afrikaans: Landery-tinktinkie, in Xhosa: Unonzwi, in Sotho: Mtantasane, in Zulu: u-Dogwe.

211. Cloud Cisticola *Cisticola textrix* 10 cm R631

Field Identification: Crown, rump and upper tail-coverts brownish buff streaked with black. Hind neck, mantle and wing-coverts blackish with narrow edging of buff to the feathers. The tail is extremely short, blackish in colour and tipped with white. There is a fine mottling of black and pale buff around and below the eye area, and the offwhite underparts are streaked with black. Eyes hazel, bill grey above, horn below, legs pinkish flesh. During the non-breeding season the black centres to the feathers become narrower and the bird appears more streaked than mottled. Females are like males in non-breeding plumage and young birds are tinted with yellow below.

Distribution: Favours flat bare marshy ground or areas with very short grass, especially near the sea at the mouths of rivers.

Notes: Not as common in the south western Cape as further north. In this area nesting takes place from August to November and the male makes remarkable display flights, rising from the ground to a height where he is almost invisible. He then makes sweeping circles uttering a loud call like 'see-see-seesee-chick-chick-chick' which is repeated every few seconds on the upward swoop. He descends in a headlong dive checking the fall before reaching the ground and landing quite gently. Does not snap its wings as it descends as other species do. The round nest is almost on the ground and covered with interwoven green grass blades. Eggs number four and are pale green, speckled with brown. In Afrikaans: Gevlekte Klopkloppie.

212. Neddicky *Cisticola fulvicapilla* 10 cm R637

Field Identification: Forehead, crown and nape chestnut, with the rest of the upper parts, including the rounded fanshaped tail, a dull brown. Sides of face buff with a lighter eyebrow stripe, underparts palest grey. Eyes hazel, bill pinkish horn, legs flesh coloured.

Distribution: Found on mountain slopes, especially in fynbos and seems to show a preference for breeding in pines.

Notes: A very common resident seen singly or in pairs. When the breeding season arrives the male finds a particular song-perch and repeats his song, which is a loud resonant 'weep-weep-weep-weep' which rises in pitch and volume. This is repeated all day long. If disturbed and alarmed the Neddicky will fly into a bush or other hiding place and observe the intruder intently from his new shelter. The breeding season in the Cape is from September to December, when an oval nest, made from broad grass blades, will be found in a tuft of grass. It will be lined with fine soft vegetable matter and contain from three to five eggs varying in colour. They could be bluish, greenish or pure white, marked with varying pattern of red. In Afrikaans: Neddikkie, in Xhosa: Incede, in Zulu: u-Gigi or i-Ncede.

213. Greybacked Cisticola *Cisticola subruficapilla* 12 cm R638

Field Identification: The forehead and crown are reddish brown, streaked with black, the back grey streaked with black, the rump greyish brown, the large tail brown with black subterminal spots seen both from above and below, and narrowly tipped with offwhite. Flight feathers are tawny, underparts pale grey, eyes brown, bill pinky grey, legs pink. Females are the same and young birds have faces washed with yellow.

Distribution: The characteristic cisticola of the Cape Flats and abundant in all types of indigenous bush except Fynbos. Found on coastal sand-dunes, estuarine flats and in Karoo-type habitats.

Notes: A common species of the drier western parts with a loud ringing call 'proueeee-tseep-tseep-tseep'. During the breeding season from August to November a descending melodic song is heard, sometimes introduced with a rapid uttering of confused notes, and the alarm call is a reedy 'tee-tee-tee' or a grating 'churr'. The round ball-shaped nest is usually placed low down in a bush, well hidden in grass, and contains three or four pale blue eggs, freckled in reddish, brown or purple. In Afrikaans: Grysrug-tinktinkie.

214. Levaillant's Cisticola *Cisticola tinniens* 13 cm R646

Field Identification: Forehead, crown and nape warm russet brown. Mantle, scapulars and wing-coverts black with feathers edged with buff. Flight feathers russet. Sides of face, stripe over eye, and underparts buff, with throat offwhite. Tail feathers blackish with broad russet edges and all but the centre feathers tipped with offwhite. Eyes brown, bill black, legs greyish flesh. Female similar but usually more dappled on nape. During the winter months the crown becomes streaked. Young birds have the appearance of adults in winter plumage, but are usually more heavily streaked and have yellow shading on face and breast.

Distribution: Resident and common in marshy places, especially the short reeds or weeds on the edges of such areas.

Notes: Usually found in pairs flitting just above marshy vegetation, with a jerky flight pattern and much flicking of the tail. When disturbed will sound the alarm call, which is a fairly loud 'tee-tee-tee' uttered as they select the highest available perch from which to watch the intruder, or otherwise fly over the one who is causing the disturbance. The call during the breeding season starts with a soft 'chee-chee' and then swells into a loud warbling 'cher-rueee'. Eggs are laid from August to October in the Cape, and vary considerably in colour. They number three, four or five and can be white, greenish, or bluish, spotted with reds or greys. The nest is found in the weeds or reeds around marshy areas and is oval-shaped, usually being made of rootlets and grass, and lined with plant down. Occasionally the whole nest is made of down. In Afrikaans: Vleitinktinkie.

215. Karoo Prinia *Prinia maculosa* 14 cm R651

Field Identification: The offwhite breast and chin are heavily streaked with black, and the brown tail is rather long and thin; these two factors would be the most distinctive characteristics. All upper parts are a medium greyish brown. The eye area is pale buff above and below the eye, finely speckled with brown. The tail viewed from below in flight shows four pairs of blackish spots arranged along each edge from base to tip. Eyes light brown, bill black, legs and feet pink. Females are similar and young birds are even more heavily streaked, the markings being rather more dusky than black.

Distribution: Abundant in indigenous bush, coastal scrub, on mountain slopes and near streams.

Notes: A noisy species usually found in pairs and small parties, creeping around in the undergrowth looking for food. The long tail is characteristically flicked up and down. They are excitable little birds and if disturbed will take up a prominent position to watch the intruder, uttering a loud scolding noise all the while. If pursued will slip into the depths of the vegetation and make an escape on the other side. Males have a dipping display flight during the breeding season, which is from August to December, with a decided peak in September. During this flight he will dip and thud his wings while uttering a loud 'cheenk-cheenk'. The nest is usually in a low bush and, as can be seen in the photograph is constructed from grass and plant down, as well as a white woolly plant down. It is roughly oval in shape with the entrance on the side. Two to five bluish-white eggs, spotted with brown, lilac and black are laid. In Afrikaans: Karoo-langstert-tinktinkie.

216. Spotted Flycatcher *Muscicapa striata* 14 cm R654

Field Identification: Slightly larger than the Dusky Flycatcher. All upper parts including the wings and tail are ash brown, with the forehead crown and nape marked with black and offwhite. Underparts are offwhite with sides of throat and chest streaked with ash brown. Eyes dark brown, bill black, legs ash brown. Sexes are alike.

Distribution: A common non-breeding summer visitor from the Palaearctic, sparingly distributed as far south as the south western Cape. Occasionally reaches the vicinity of Cape Town but is more frequent near Somerset West. Usually found singly, perched low on bare branches. Is known to return to the same area year after year. Picture of nesting bird taken in Europe.

Notes: Recorded from late September to early April, and will be seen using its perch, bordering open spaces, from which to dart at insects in flight. Has a characteristic habit of flicking out its wings halfway when perched. The call is a thin reedy 'tzee', and if alarmed, a sharp 'tec-tec' or a fast repeated 'tzee'tuc-tuc'. In Afrikaans: Europese Vlieëvanger.

217. Dusky Flycatcher *Muscicapa adusta* 12 cm R655

Field Identification: Smaller and greyer than the Spotted Flycatcher, and with less distinct markings. Upper parts, including wings and tail, mousy grey, with flight feathers a little darker. Eyestripe, above and below the eye, as well as throat whitish, underparts offwhite, streaked over chest and sides with ash brown. Eyes dark brown, bill black, legs dark grey. Females are similar and young birds are heavily spotted with buffish marking on upper parts, and more mottled on chest. Nestlings can be seen in the nest.

Distribution: A woodland bird inhabiting indigenous forests as well as oak and mixed woodlands. A few are resident but most are migratory, moving northwards to Natal and Mozambique during the winter months.

Notes: Found usually singly or in pairs under big trees, perched fairly low down and darting spasmodically at insects. Has a habit of flicking its wings when perched, like the Spotted Flycatcher. Would often go unnoticed if it were not for its quiet call 'tsi-rit-tsirit-tsirit'. Breeding takes place from September to January and the nest is to be found in a variety of places, from moss-covered rocks to holes in banks, to the

branches of a tree. This particular bird appears to have chosen an indentation in a bank to build the nest, which is neatly constructed from fibres, roots and mosses, and lined with feathers, rootlets or even horse hair if available. Eggs usually number three, and are greenish white, speckled with pinkish to brownish spots. In Afrikaans: Donker Vlieëvanger.

218. Chestnutvented Titbabbler
Parisoma subcaeruleum **15 cm R658**

Field Identification: The rufous under tail-coverts are a clear distinguishing feature, also the plumage of the alula is tipped with white, forming a distinct pattern on the wing shoulder on the folded wing, clearly seen in the photograph. Upper parts including the wings are dark grey, with chin and throat offwhite, heavily streaked with black, underparts lighter grey. The tail is black with all but the central feathers tipped with white. Eyes are white or cream, bill black, legs dark grey. The female is duller and young birds have less streaks on the throat.
Distribution: Regular in Strandveld and coastal Renosterbosveld. Found creeping around in thickets and thorn trees, especially in dongas or on sheltered hillsides. A common resident species.
Notes: Found singly or in pairs. Usually keeps out of sight searching thoroughly through thickets for insects before leaving that spot to search a neighbouring tree or bush. Food is derived from spiders, insects, grubs and berries. Often imitates the call of other birds but has an individual call like an explosive run of sharply uttered 'ticks', followed by clear melodic notes like 'chuu-ti-chuuti-chuu-chuu'. When feeding they utter a loud 'cheriktiktik' which is answered similarly by the mate. Breeding takes place from August to December, but more often in August and September. The

nest will usually be about a metre from the ground in thick vegetation, but placed near the end of a branch. As can be seen in the photograph, it is bowl-shaped and delicately made from fibre and rootlets, held together with cobwebs and twigs, and lined with fine plant-down or dry grass. Eggs usually number two or three, white with greenish brown, sepia, and blue-grey markings. In Afrikaans: Tjeriktik.

219. Fiscal Flycatcher *Sigelus silens* 19 cm R665

Field Identification: Sometimes confused with the Fiscal Shrike but this species has a much shorter black tail, which when spread out is fan-shaped and shows two white patches, one on either side, on the outer tail feathers. The adult male has all upper parts a glossy black, with white patches on primaries and secondaries. The throat and sides of neck are offwhite, with chest and belly light grey. Eyes dark brown, bill and legs black. The female has the black replaced by blackish brown, immature birds are spotted above and mottled below but have the same wing and tail pattern as adult birds. Small dark nestlings can be seen in the nest.

Distribution: Found along tree-lined rivers and in indigenous bush, especially coastal Macchia.

Notes: Common and resident where there are large bushes, and usually found in pairs. Not very active and often seen on some prominent perch used as a lookout for hawking insects in open country or in the gardens of towns. The diet is made up mainly of insects, but on occasion they will eat seeds and fruit as well. The cry is a drawnout feeble 'wheeze' followed by 'chat-chat' or when alarmed, a sharp 'skisk' or 'kirr-kirr-kirr'. Breeding is from August to November, with a peak in September. The nest is often found at the base of an aloe leaf, or in the fork of a small tree. It is a bowl-shaped structure made of rootlets, twigs, weeds and straw – and what appears to be a piece of rope as well in this particular nest. It is lined with soft vegetable down and usually contains two to four pale greenish blue eggs, finely speckled with reddish at the thicker end. In Afrikaans: Fiskaal-vlieëvanger, in Xhosa: Icola.

220. Cape Batis *Batis capensis* 12 cm R672

Field Identification: The adult male has a dark grey forehead, crown and nape, with a wide black line running from the black bill, over the eye area and to the side of the hind neck. Chin, throat and sides of neck are white, with a broad, though variable, black band around the chest. The mantle and rump are an olive-washed grey and the wings are dark grey with rufous wing coverts, seen as a patch when the wings are folded. The flanks are rufous, underparts white, and the black tail is narrowly edged with white. eyes are yellow, but red during the breeding season, legs black. The female, seen on the nest, has a fine white line at the edge of the grey crown, from the bill and over the dark brown eye, the chin and throat are rufous with white only at the sides, and around the sides of the neck. The band around the upper chest is chestnut and not black as in the male bird. Immature birds are grey above, streaked with buff, the throat is tinged with buff and the underparts are white.
Distribution: A species common to moister forests and kloofs and the marginal vegetation of these areas.

Notes: Active and excitable, usually found in pairs and often in company with other species, searching for insects in the branches of trees or flying out to catch insects in the air. In this magnificent photograph of a Cape Batis pair it would appear that the male has fed the female on the nest a spider and there seems to be a minor problem with the web. They are known to be very tame during the incubating period and will allow observers to come very close. When disturbed and alarmed they have a characteristic way of making a whirring noise with their wings. The usual call is a monotonously repeated 'reep-reep-reep'; the alarm note is a harsh 'prritt-pritt' and another call is a softer 'wee-warrawarra'. Breeding takes place from September to December and two or three greenish or pinkish white eggs, with greyish brown and reddish brown blotches, will be found in a neat bowl-shaped nest of fibrous vegetation. In Afrikaans: Bosbontrokkie, in Xhosa: in-Gedle.

221. Fairy Warbler *Stenostira scita* 12 cm R678

Field Identification: Upper parts are dark grey with a black patch on the side of the head from the black bill, over the eye area, and including the ear-coverts, above which is a thin white eyebrow stripe. There is a thin white moustache stripe and offwhite chin, sometimes washed with pink. Wings are blackish grey with a blue tinge, and the white wing-coverts and inner secondaries form a white line on the wing when folded. Throat and upper chest bluish grey, belly whitish with a pink wash, underparts light grey. The fairly long tail is black with all but the central feathers being white-tipped, and with the outermost feathers white. Eyes dark brown, legs black. Females are similar and immature birds are lighter and browner above, usually lacking the pink on belly.

Distribution: Common to the drier areas. Occurs in the Verloren Vlei and Cogmanskloof areas and northward as a resident. Has also been recorded as far south as Gordon's Bay.

Notes: Not seen easily as it is inclined to search for insects by creeping around in trees and vegetation. The call has been described as being like the 'kiss-kiss-kiss-kiss' of a sunbird, and a further call sounds like 'cheep-cheep'. Breeding takes place from August to October in the Cape, and the nest, which takes four days for the female to build, is made of fine grass and twigs, lined with vegetable down or the

hair of animals. The outside of the nest is often covered with cobwebs and lichen. Two or three cream coloured eggs are laid, which are tinged with green and finely speckled. In Afrikaans: Fee-vlieëvanger.

222. Paradise Flycatcher *Terpsiphone viridis* 20 cm R682

Field Identification: A spectacular bird when in breeding plumage, especially the male, with the two central elongated chestnut-red tail feathers. The crested head, nape and throat are deep metallic blue, with the wattle round the reddish-brown eyes, and a portion of the black bill, a bright cobalt blue. Chest and belly dark grey with underparts grey. The mantle is brilliant reddish chestnut, as are the wings and tail plumage, with flight feathers rather more dusky. The photograph shows the white under wing-coverts. Legs are grey. The female lacks some of the metallic sheen on the head, underparts are rather more white, and the tail lacks the two elongated central feathers. Immature birds resemble the female. Nestlings are

brownish grey, as seen in the nest.

Distribution: A summer migrant to the south western Cape, favouring dense vegetation along streams, and partial to inhabiting oaks and mixed exotics. Fairly tame and often found in private gardens.

Notes: Usually seen in pairs hunting insects on the wing, and being made very conspicuous due to the long tail of the male streaming behind in an undulating flight. The short calls, 'ziza', 'swee-swer' and 'zwa-i-zwer' are like the calls of the Bluemantled Flycatcher inhabiting the eastern parts of South Africa. Breeds from October to December, with a peak in November. The nest is found in the fork of a tree and its neat bowl-shaped structure of bark and fibres is disguised on the ouside with lichens, seen clearly in the photograph. This camouflage is betrayed however, and the whereabouts of the three creamy

pink-tinted, chestnut-spotted eggs is revealed, by the waving chestnut tail of the male, who assists with the incubation and feeding of the young birds. In Afrikaans: Paradys-vlieëvanger, in Xhosa: Ujejane, in Zulu: Uve, in Sotho: mo-Thoapea.

223. African Pied Wagtail *Motacilla aguimp* 20 cm R685

Field Identification: Adult male black above, from black bill, over head, nape, mantle, rump and tail, the latter having a white edge down both sides. There is a very distinct broad white eyebrow from bill to nape, and a black biblike band dipping across the upper chest, contrasting with the white throat, sides of neck and lower chest, flanks and underparts washed with grey. The wings are mainly black but the upper wing-coverts are white, and the flight feathers have white spots and edges, so that when the wings are folded there is a great deal of white showing. Eyes brown, legs blackish grey. The female is a duller, less glossy black and young birds are brownish with white wing coverts which distinguish them from young Cape Wagtails.

Distribution: Rare in the south western Cape, where vagrant visitors have been recorded from Zeekoe Vlei, Gordon's Bay in April and May, and from Saldanha Bay.

Notes: Found in pairs near water, frequenting the sandbanks and rocks of larger rivers. Fairly tame, not being unduly disturbed by onlookers as they feed on insects

along the bank. Has a fairly melodic song and a shriller short 'tu-whee'. The nest is a bulky, loosely constructed structure containing a neat cup of fine grass and feathers, with three or four eggs coloured offwhite with sepia and grey markings. This species is however a very rare visitor to the area and nesting has been recorded only at Gordon's Bay. In Afrikaans: Bont Kwikstert, in Zulu: um-Vemve, in Xhosa: um-Celu, in Sotho: mo-Selakatane.

224. Cape Wagtail *Motacilla capensis* 18 cm R686

Field Identification: A very common little bird uniformly greyish brown above, including the wings and tail, the latter having a whitish edge down both sides. The tail is made conspicuous by its bobbing action when the bird walks along the ground.

There is a white line over the eye, a darkish band across the chest, throat white, belly and underparts a mixture of white and buff. The wing-coverts are edged with white, which forms a slight white line on the wings when folded, the secondaries are edged with light buff, flight feathers rather darker. Eyes dark brown, bill and legs greyish. The female is the same and young birds are browner above and below.

Distribution: Resident and common throughout the area within reach of water. Found in parks and gardens, in farms and near the sea.

Notes: A very tame and familiar bird that has adapted well to human habitation and is common in gardens everywhere, chasing insects on the ground and flying up to catch them when disturbed. Feed on a variety of insects and sandhoppers, as well as food scraps anywhere about the garden. Usually seen in pairs or family parties, but when not breeding will roost in large flocks especially during the winter months. Breeding takes place at any time throughout the year, with a peak in the spring, around September, nests being found in creepers, in scaffolding, in hedges, or tree stumps when near to human habitation. In the wild the usual site is in a thick tuft of grass near a river. The nest is bulky with a deep cup of fine vegetation and any available hair. The eggs, numbering two to four or occasionally more, are a dull yellow, finely speckled with brown. In Afrikaans: Kwikkie, in Sotho: mo-Tjoli, in Zulu: u-Mvemve, in Xhosa: Umventshane.

225. Richard's Pipit *Anthus novaeseelandiae* 18 cm R692

Field Identification: A tawny coloured pipit variable in colouring, being a mix of light buff and greyish brown. The head has dusky streaks on a light buff background, and a darker colouring through the eye and at the ear coverts. Back and rump are slightly darker and mottled, throat is offwhite, chest darker buff, upper chest distinctly streaked with blackish brown, belly and underparts light tawny and offwhite, tail brown with outer feathers white. In non-breeding plumage the upper parts are only lightly mottled and the edges to the wing-coverts are lighter. Eyes dark brown, bill brown above, horn below, legs pinky beige. Females are similar and young birds have the feathers of the wings and upper parts edged with white, giving a more mottled effect.

Distribution: Very common in open country especially cultivated land and open grasslands near water, or moist ground around vleis.

Notes: Spends most of its time on the ground and is found crouched on upturned sods, more rarely perched on trees or bushes. Lives on a variety of insects. The male performs a display flight in the breeding season – a circular flight pattern of dipping undulation, while uttering a loud call at each dip. The calls of Richard's Pipit are a loud 'chis-sik' or 'pip-pip' as well as a short melodic song. Breeds August to December, the nest being found on the ground next to a tuft of grass, made from dry grass, lined with small rootlets and bits of hair. the eggs usually number three and are cream coloured, freckled or streaked with sepia, brown and grey. In Afrikaans: Gewone Koester, in Xhosa: Icetshu, in Zulu: um-Ngcelu.

226. Orangethroated Longclaw *Macronyx capensis* 20 cm R703

Field Identification: Probably the most distinctive aspect for identification is the bright orange throat, outlined by the black gorget which forms a circle from the base of the black bill, down the sides of the neck and across the breast. Breast and belly are yellow, with breast streaked, and a yellow eyestripe runs over the eye. Upper parts, forehead, crown, nape, mantle, rump and wings are a mixture of lightish brown streaked with darker brown and edged with yellowish buff. Flight feathers brown with narrow yellowish edges, tail brown with four outer feathers tipped with white. Eyes are brown, legs a lighter yellowish brown. The female has a paler throat and young birds have the throat yellowish streaked with blackish spots.

Distribution: Resident and common, found in damp open lands especially coastal Macchia, coastal Renosterbosveld and pasture lands.

Notes: Seen in pairs, usually on the ground in search of beetles or grasshoppers as well as stinkbugs, termites or weevils. The flight is slow and heavy with a noisy wirring wingbeat, often accompanied by a 'mewing' call. When disturbed will not fly for a long distance and the perch is usually not higher than a tuft of grass or a low bush. Breeds from August to November, but mot often in August and September. Nests are found on the ground but more often well hidden in a tuft of grass. It is a thick structure formed from grasses and lined with rootlets, containing three or four dull creamy eggs, marked at the thicker end with brown, reddish and grey. In Afrikaans: Kalkoentjie, in Xhosa: Inqilo, in Zulu: i-Qoomfi.

227. Fiscal Shrike *Lanius collaris* 23 cm R707

Field Identification: Mainly black above and white below with rump and upper tail-coverts grey. There is a white V on the back formed by the folded scapulars, well illustrated in the photograph. The tail is graduated with shorter white-tipped feathers around the central dark ones, giving the effect of a white edge around a black tail, when folded. eyes dark brown, bill and legs black. The female has chestnut on the flanks and immature birds are ash brown above, light grey below finely barred, and with wing feathers edged with buff.

Distribution: Very common throughout the area, especially in open grasslands where trees are scattered. Does not favour heavily forested areas and is not a prolific species in Macchia.

Notes: Has adapted well to human habitation and is familiar in gardens where it is often seen on a dominant perch, on the lookout for food. A carnivorous shrike, with both sexes intolerant of any other birds in its area, and it will seek and destroy intruders, often impaling them on thorns or barbed-wire fences. Feed on a great variety of insects with a preference for beetles and grasshoppers, but will eat lizards, small snakes, frogs, chameleons, and other wild or caged birds if the opportunity arises. Prey is carried in the bill or in the claws. Breeds mainly in August and October in the Cape, sometimes from July to January. The call is a grating harsh 'chee-chee-chee'. The nest, containing about four pale cream or pale green eggs marked with a ring of olive or grey around the thicker end, will be found int he fork of a tree. It is made from twigs and grass, lined with anything from weeds and roots to bits of wool, feathers or rags. In Afrikaans: Fiskaal, in Xhosa: Inxanxadi, in Zulu: i-Lunga.

228. Southern Boubou *Laniarius ferrugineus* 23 cm R709

Field Identification: Similar in appearance to the Fiscal Shrike but quite different in habits. Forehead, crown, nape and upper back, as well as the rounded tail a fairly glossy black. The wings are black with a white band both across and down the wing.

The rump is brownish fading to golden buff, the plumage being fairly full and fluffy. Throat, chest and belly are white with flanks and underparts light cinnamon. The female is the same but duller and browner above, with throat and chest slightly washed with yellow. eyes brown, bill black, legs grey. Young birds are barred above and below, and the wing area is buff rather than white.

Distribution: Found creeping and hopping through tangled bush, especially near water. Resident in forests and mixed exotics, or in any heavy cover, including that found in private gardens.

Notes: An inquisitive species that will come to investigate any strange noises but will remain in a concealed position. In gardens one often hears the duet calls of a pair of Boubous uttered from some thick shrubbery. Often it is a 'koko' from the male followed by a 'weet' from the female. The alarm call is a harsh 'chirr'. Breeds from September to December. If one manages to find the well concealed nest in some dense vegetation, where it is often sited, it is a shallow basin of fine twigs and roots, with or without a lining of fine grass. The eggs, usually three, are very pale green, with a ring of fine speckles in brown and grey at the larger end. In Afrikaans: Waterfiskaal, in Xhosa: Igzubusha, in Zulu: i-Boboni, in Sotho: Pzempzete.

229. Olive Bush Shrike *Telophorous olivaceus* 18 cm R717

Field Identification: Upper parts olive green with broad black mark through eye area and down sides of head to neck, above which is a thin buff eyebrow line. There is further buff between the eye and the black bill; throat, chest, and belly cinnamon with lower belly and underparts olive green, tail lighter olive. Eyes vary from pale to dark brown, legs grey. Another phase has forehead, crown and nape grey. The female is duller with the black mark on the side of the head a pale brownish colour and underparts more dull yellow than cinnamon. Immature birds are mottled above and barred below.

Distribution: Rare in the south western Cape but there are records of sightings from Somerset West, Swellendam and near Bredasdorp. Favours large evergreen forests from Sir Lowry's Pass eastwards.

Notes: This species is inclined to remain hidden in vegetation but is nevertheless inquisitive. Usually found in pairs in larger trees. Feeds on insects. The call is a high clear note followed by six rapidly repeated notes at a much lower pitch, otherwise a pretty trilling sound is uttered. Breeding takes place from October to January the nest being a fairly flimsy structure of roots and other bits of vegetation containing two very pale greenish eggs, with elongated markings of purplish brown and bluish grey. In Afrikaans: Olyf Boslaksman, in Xhosa: Umthethi.

230. Bokmakierie *Telophorus zeylonus* 23 cm R722

Field Identification: Forehead, crown, sides of head and nape grey, eyestripe, throat, chest and belly bright yellow, with a wide black biblike band around the throat extending upwards on the sides of the neck to the base of the thick black bill. Upper parts are greyish olive with flight feathers dusky, edged with yellowish green. The central tail feathers are black, with a greenish tinge, and the remaining outer tail feathers are black with broad yellow tips. Eyes dark brown, legs grey. The sexes are alike and young birds have a greenish crown, the throat is greyer and underparts are buff washed with green.

Distribution: A common resident wherever there are bushes. Not found in forests and not particularly prevalent in Macchia.

Notes: Fairly terrestrial in habits, usually seen running around bushy haunts on the ground, looking for insects, or perched in nearby bushes and trees. A beautiful bird with a lovely call well known in home gardens. Feeds on insects, spiders, chameleons, smallish lizards, caterpillars and small frogs. The familiar 'bokmakierie' or 'kokoveet' is uttered in loud clear duets with the mate, and the softer 'tok-tok-tok' or 'kwirr'kirr'kr' is the alarm call. The most usual breeding time is August but this period can extend from June to November. When they are available a preference is shown for green asparagus leaves on the outside of the nest. It is a compact basin shaped structure constructed from twigs, roots and grass, usually well hidden in vegetation. Three or four greenish blue eggs with scattered brownish spots are laid. In Afrikaans: Bok-makierie, in Xhosa: i-Ngqwani, in Sotho: Pjempjete.

231. European Starling *Sturnus vulgaris* 20 cm R733

Field Identification: The adult male has head, nape and underparts blackish green shot with iridescent green and violet above, and with a blue-black sheen below; mantle, wings and rump evenly spotted with buff. Flight feathers are blackish with narrow edges of buff, eyes dark brown, bill horn, legs pinkish. The female lacks the degree of brilliant iridescence present in the male and the dark chest and belly are spotted in offwhite, head and neck spotted with buff. Young birds are brownish above with throat whitish, speckled with brown.

Distribution: Introduced to Cape Town by Cecil Rhodes in 1899 and has spread eastwards to East London, northwards up the western coast to the S.W. African border, as well as to the King William's Town area. Now abundant near human habitation and seen stalking around garden lawns and raiding fruit trees. Thought to drive indigenous birds away.

Notes: Very noisy when roosting in flocks on buildings or in tall trees at night. Huge flocks form in winter, very often with Cape Weavers. Food is derived from insects and soft fruit. The peak of the breeding season is October, but can take place from September to November. A favoured nesting site is in holes under the eaves of houses – unpopular because they are said to introduce a form of 'lice' into the build-

ing. The normal call is a grating, lively, creaking chatter, as well as an imitation of the calls of other birds. The nest hole is sparsely lined with a few pine needles of a few bits of grass and three to five pale blue eggs are laid. In Afrikaans: Europese Spreeu.

232. Wattled Starling *Creatophora cinerea* 21 cm R735

Field Identification: The mature male when non-breeding is greyish beige above with bare black streaks on both sides of the throat. The rump is lighter and the wing flight feathers, and tail plumage, is blackish brown, all clearly seen in the photograph. When breeding the head is bare and black with black wattles on crown, forehead and throat, and with a section of the bare skin on the crown yellow. Eyes are dark brown, bill pinkish horn, legs pinkish brown. Females resemble the non-breeding male and immature birds resemble the female except that young females are browner than young males.

Distribution: A rare visitor in the south western parts, but more numerous and locally abundant in

the more eastern areas such as Bredasdorp and towards Hopefield in the northern parts.

Notes: Inclined to move about restlessly either in small parties or in large flocks and will follow locust swarms. Other food is derived from snails, termites, grasshoppers and crickets, as well as fruit. Nests colonially in huge flocks usually where locusts have laid their eggs. When these hatch they form a good supply of food but if the supply fails for some reason, adult birds will abandon eggs and nestlings and move off in search of food elsewhere. Nests are made from thorny twigs and sticks and may be double or treble nests, with perhaps dozens of these in one thorn bush. If food and rain is abundant four eggs are laid, but should food be short, or drought conditions prevalent, only three eggs are laid. the eggs are pale greenish blue sparsely speckled. In Afrikaans: Lel-spreeu, in Xhosa: Uwambu, in Zulu: i-Ntetengwane, in Sotho: le-Fokori.

233. Palewinged Starling *Onychognathus nabouroup* 27 cm R744

Field Identification: A rather large glossy blue-black starling with a faint green sheen on the head and neck and two thirds of the primary flight feathers light chestnut to white, which appear as large whitish 'windows' in the wings when in flight, and as light bars on the folded wings, seen clearly in the photograph. Eyes orange red, bill and legs black. The female is similar but smaller.

Distribution: Fairly common in the dry Clanwilliam area but not recorded further south except from Robertson and Worcester.

Notes: A species inhabiting rocky hill and mountain areas, usually found in flocks or at least small parties. Live on a mixed diet of insects, berries and fruit. The nest, a flattish basin of grass and plant stems, is found in the crevices of precipii and contains three or four pale greenish blue eggs, slightly speckled with a reddish brown. In Afrikaans: Bleekvlerk-spreeu.

234. Redwinged Starling *Onychognathus morio* 27 cm R745

Field Identification: Similar to the previous species in appearance except that the windows in the wings are a deep reddish chestnut. The general colour is a glossy blue-black with a greenish tinge on the sides of head, wings and tail, so beautifully illustrated in the photograph of both the male and the female together. Eyes are dark brown, bill and legs black. The female has the head, neck, and upper chest streaked with grey and young birds are sooty black.

Distribution: A common species of hilly and mountainous country but may also be seen far from rocky krantzes, when foraging for food.

Notes: Occur in pairs or in large roving flocks that will enter towns and raid gardens. Feed on indigenous berries and a wide variety of fruits, such as plums, figs, apricots and grapes. Caterpillars, earthworms, millipedes, termites and stick insects are also eaten in fair amounts, and this species will also probe flowers for nectar, and have been seen perched on animals while eating ticks – an amazingly varied diet. A mournful whistle is often uttered while in flight, and the pattern of flight is characterised by a constant dipping. The chestnut patch on the wings is clearly evident at that time. When alarmed by an intruder a sharp 'tchorr' is uttered. Breeds from September to December in the Cape. The nest is a basin of grass and sticks plastered with mud and lined with horsehair. Eggs number three to five and are pale greenish blue, slightly spotted with red. In Afrikaans: Rooivlerkspreeu, in Zulu: in-Somi, in Xhosa: Isomi.

235. Pied Starling *Spreo bicolor* 26 cm R746

Field Identification: A rich brownish black with a slight bronze and green sheen. Under tail-coverts and lower belly white or sometimes palest buff. Eyes palest yellow or white, gape yellow, bill black with base half of the lower mandible yellow, legs black. Sexes are alike and young birds have the base of the bill buff.

Distribution: This species is becoming increasingly rarer in the fruit producing areas, but is still a common resident throughout the south western Cape except in very thick bush or forest, on the larger mountains and in the city of Cape Town.

Notes: A gregarious starling found feeding on ants as well as a certain amount of crickets, beetles and grubs. Has a typical upright stance when walking about among cattle where it eats grasshoppers disturbed by the animals, or picks ticks off the animals. The call is a fairly soft 'gwah-i-gwah-i' uttered in flight, and the alarm call is a harsh, grating hiss. Breeding takes place from August to November, with a marked peak in September. The nest is a hole in a bank or dry river bed, or could be under an eaves. When burrowed in a bank it is about a meter in, and the well padded nest contains four to six bluish green eggs, half plain, and half spotted with reddish brown. In Afrikaans: Witgat-spreeu, in Zulu: i-Gwayigwayi, in Xhosa: i-Giyogiyo, in Sotho: le-Holi.

236. Cape Sugarbird *Promerops cafer* 44 cm R749

Field Identification: The male, with his extremely long tail, is much longer than the female. Forehead and crown are buff, finely streaked with brown, the brown streaking also forming a darker line from the bill through the eye and to the neck. Mantle and wings are brown and dusky, the rump greenish yellow with dusky streaks. Throat is whitish, neck and upper chest russet, belly offwhite, under tail-coverts yellow, all streaked with dusky, tail dusky brown. The long thin bill is black, eyes dark brown, legs black. Immature birds have short tails.

Distribution: During the breeding season from February to August this species is found on the mountains, but later in the year they move from this habitat according to the available food supply. They favour areas where proteas are in bloom, as this lovely picture verifies.

Notes: The Cape Sugarbird was previously believed to be closely related to the Australian honeyeater but through research it is now known to be closely related to the Starlings. The habit of individually moving into a low bush, and then flying in groups of five or six to a large communal roosting tree, where five hundred or more birds may congregate, and using this site during an entire season, is also similar to the behaviour of starlings, as is the habit of sitting on a high perch and chortling. They will remain in this roost until well after sunrise. Breeding, however, is not communal. the male is seen perched on the tops of bushes, with his long tail fluttering in the wind, calling and singing, but stopping intermittently to ward off other intruding males. He puts on a courtship performance with his long tail feathers held over his back and much wing clapping during the display and also bobs up and down with the tail hanging straight down. Food is derived from insects and from the nectar of protea blooms. The nest is constructed by the female of dead twigs and grass, softly lined with vegetable fibres and down from proteas. It is usually found fairly high up in a protea bush. Eggs usually number two and vary from buff to brown, marked with purplish black, or finer spots and lines in brown. In Afrikaans: Suikervoël.

237. Malachite Sunbird *Nectarinia famosa* 24 cm R751

Field Identification: In breeding plumage the male has head, neck, mantle and chest a brilliant metallic green tinged with gold. Flight feathers and tail, with two elongated central feathers, dusky black, pectoral tufts bright yellow. Eyes dark brown, long thin curved bill black, legs black. By comparison the female is drab, forehead and crown lightly mottled with ash brown and greyish beige; mantle, back and rump greyish, short tail and wings darker. Chin, throat, and chest yellowish beige streaked with ash brown, belly and underparts yellowish beige. The male during the non-breeding season much resembles the female but retains some of the metallic colouring on the wing-coverts, the rump and upper tail-coverts. The long central tail feathers may also be retained for much of that period. Immature birds resemble the female.
Distribution: Sometimes found in gardens but prefers open country side and indigenous vegetation. A widely distributed common resident species.
Notes: The male is very noticeable, either flying very fast chasing other males, or sitting on a conspicuous perch, such as the head of an aloe, uttering its loud calls – a clear 'chipp' or a rapid succession 'chip-chip-chip' or a songlike 'chee-chee-twistee-

twistee'. Insects are caught in flight and food is also derived from the nectar of Aloes, Kniphofia and Leonotis. Spiders and small moths are eaten as well. During the display flights the male swoops downwards towards the female displaying his bright yellow pectoral tufts. Breeds from June to December, especially in July and August. The nest is the typical oval-shaped grass struc-ture of the Sunbirds and is usually found over water or on the bank of a dry gully, strength-ened with twigs and leaves from the plant in which it is built. Plant down forms the lining and it will usually contain two eggs which are cream, heavily mottled with olive, brown and grey. In Afri-kaans: Jangroentjie, in Xhosa: Ingcumgcu, in Zulu: Ncwincwi, in Sotho: Tsekhane.

♀

238. Orangebreasted Sunbird *Nectarinia violacea* 15 cm R753

Field Identification: A wonderful picture of the magnificently colourful male with entire head, neck, throat and mantle brilliant metallic green. A band of deep purple separates the neck from the bright golden breast, with belly and lower parts bright cinnamon yellow. The lower back is yellowish olive, the wings blackish, with yellow edges, and the tail, with very elongated central feathers, black. Females are more yellowish green than females of the Lesser Doublecollared Sunbird, but are nevertheless drab with the overall colouring being a dull pale yellowish green, upper parts mottled with ashy brown and flight feathers and short tail more dusky brown. Immature birds resemble the female. eyes dark brown, long bill and legs black.

Distribution: Endemic to the south western Cape and confined mainly to the fynbos areas where it is resident and breeding.

Notes: Seen most often in pairs where heaths and proteas abound, either at the coast or even to the tops of mountains throughout the area. They appear oblivious to the harshest climatic conditions. Feed on nectar from ericas and protea, as well as on insects such as flies and spiders. The males are especially noisy and active, the call being a harsh 'tsearp' or a 'teer-turp' repeated twice. Breeding takes place from May to August, and the nest, made by the female, is constructed from a mixture of twigs, grass and down from proteas, well insulated against the cold and rainy conditions typical of the Cape winter. Eggs number one or two and are white with a freckling of greyish brown. In Afrikaans: Oranjebors-suikerbekkie.

239. Greater Doublecollared Sunbird
Nectarinia afra 14 cm R758

Field Identification: The adult male has entire head, throat and mantle a brilliant metallic green, with a very broad band of bright scarlet across the chest, separated from the throat colouring by a narrow band of iridescent violet blue, underparts brown, wings and tail blackish brown. Greatly resembles the Lesser Doublecollared Sunbird but it is a larger species, the bill is heavier and the scarlet chestband is about twice as wide. Eyes dark brown, bill and legs black. the female is blackish brown above and lighter greyish brown below, immature birds resemble the female.

Distribution: Rare in the south western Cape, usually eastward from Swellendam, but definitely known from Robertson, Caledon, De Wet, the Helderberg and the Hottentots Holland.

Notes: Subject to local fluctuations in numbers, and during the non-breeding season will be found in small parties. Feeds on a variety of insects, the nectar from aloes and other flowers, as well as the juice from soft, ripe fruits. The male has a warbling song, a courtship call 'chert-chert' and other calls like 'skiz-skiz' and 'cheet-cheet'. The nest is suspended at the end of branches,

208

or on vines hanging in krantzes, and is built by the female. One or two eggs are laid, white with thin cloudy markings in olive, grey and brown. In Afrikaans: Groot Rooibors-suikerbekkie, in Xhosa: Ingcungcu.

240. Lesser Doublecollared Sunbird
Nectarinia chalybea **12 cm R760**

Field Identification: The male has head, neck, mantle and upper chest bright metallic limy green with a golden sheen, a darkish shading on the hind neck, and a narrow band of brilliant blue across the centre chest, below which is a band of bright scarlet, belly and underparts ashy buff. Rump blue, flight and tail feathers brown, eyes dark brown, bill and legs black. The female is a rather pale ash grey with darker flight and tail feathers. Young birds are like the female but are usually darker.
Distribution: This is the most numerous species of sunbird in the south western Cape except in Maccia. Resident though with local movement in places. Up to 1978 birds in the central areas moved into the Cape Flats, Strandfontein area, to breed, but now breed locally. Found wherever there are trees, as well as in scrub or forests.
Notes: Flight is very rapid and is characterised by a great deal of swerving. The call is a high-pitched rapid 'cheep-cheep' as well as a pleasant little song used mainly during the courtship display. Feeds on the nectar of a variety of flowers, as well as larvae, beetles, spiders and flies. The nest is built by the female and hangs from a fairly

high branch in a bush or tree. It is constructed from a variety of plant materials and cobwebs, lined with plant down or feathers. Breeding takes place from April to November and eggs usually number two. They are cream, heavily mottled with brown, grey or blackish spots or lines. In Afrikaans: Klein Rooibors-suikerbekkie, in Xhosa: Ingcumgcu.

241. Dusky Sunbird *Nectarinia fusca* 11 cm R764

Field Identification: Upperparts, forehead, crown, nape, and back, medium brown with darker brown, tail blackish. Chin to upper belly black, pectoral tufts bright orange, lower belly and underparts white. eyes dark brown, bill and legs black. The female is light ash grey above, whitish below tinged with buff, flight feathers and tail dusky brown – similar to the female Lesser Doublecollared Sunbird but somewhat paler. Immature birds resemble the female, though tinged with yellow above and below, and young males have black throats.

Distribution: Essentially a karoo species occurring mainly in drought years. During the spring and early summer of 1978, which followed a very dry winter, there was an invasion of this species in the Peninsula and surrounding areas. Recorded from the Olifants River, Montagu and Robertson under normal circumstances. Found in dry or arid country and in the valleys of dry rivers.

Notes: Locally common where food is plentiful, feeding on insects and their larvae, as well as at the flowers of aloes as seen in the photograph. Rather inconspicuous and fairly quiet, with a harsh call, 'chrr-chek-chek' and a twittering call when feeding. The nest is most often found in a euphorbia or prickly pear plant, but could be slung from some bush. It is made of grass, leaves and fibres, lined with down and feathers if available. This species is inclined to build nests which are rejected and build further nests. Breeding takes place from August to March when two or three eggs are laid. They have a white background and are marked, mainly at the thicker end, with blue, brown and purple. In Afrikaans: Namakwa Suikerbekkie.

210

242. Black Sunbird *Nectarinia amethystina* 15 cm R772

Field Identification: The adult male is easily distinguished by the bright metallic purple on the sides of the neck, as well as on the upper tail coverts and the wing shoulder. Forehead and crown are bright metallic green, the rest of the plumage black with a soft goldish purple iridescence on the wing plumage. The long, curved bill is black as are the legs, with eyes dark brown. Females are olivy brown above, including the sides of the head and neck, with wing and tail plumage a darker dusky brown. Underparts from chin to lower belly are light sandy beige, streaked heavily with blackish brown on throat, and with lighter streaks towards the lower chest and belly. Young birds are similar to the female, but darker on the throat and tinged with yellow below.

Distribution: Not usually found further west than Swellendam although it does occur in the Overberg. Inhabits the more open forested areas and is found in gardens in built-up areas.

Notes: A common sunbird found in pairs during the breeding season or in small parties when non-breeding. Has a loud persistent call which is a high-pitched 'tseet' and a staccato 'chi-chi-chi', but when alarmed by an intruder will utter a quick 'tit-tit-tit'. Usually seen foraging busily for food in the form of spiders, aphids, termites and a variety of flying insects, as well as the nectar of aloes and other flowers. Will readily attack other species. Breeds from August to March, the nest being a pear shaped structure suspended from a tall tree, usually containing two white or cream eggs, with elongated grey and brown markings. In Afrikaans: Swart Suikerbekkie, in Xhosa: Ingcungcu.

243. Cape White-eye *Zosterops pallidus* 13 cm R775

Field Identification: Upper parts are dull greenish yellow, throat brighter yellow, and underparts varying in degree of grey, beige, white, and yellow with beige. The brown eye is edged all round with a distinct white ring, bill and legs are black. As can be seen from the picture of the pair of Cape White-eyes, the female resembles the male. Young birds are duller and do not develop the white eye ring until they are five weeks old.

Distribution: A very common resident found in forests, thick indigenous bush, plantations and cultivated gardens.

Notes: Have a type of follow-on' pattern of flight as they follow each other, as they ransack tree after tree in search of food. This species favours soft fruits, such as ripe figs, berries, insects and a sugary substance exuded by aphids in winter. Are known to venture on to outside tables where teas are served, and take sugar from the sugar bowls. Form loose flocks during the non-breeding season which break up when they form pairs for breeding, which is from September to December. The nest is cup shaped, formed from fine straw and fibres, and covered with moss and cobwebs. It is found attached to the outer twigs of branches. Eggs number two or three and are either white or pale blue. In Afrikaans: Kaapse Witogie, in Xhosa: Intukwane.

244. House Sparrow *Passer domesticus* 15 cm R784

Field Identification: The adult male has forehead, crown, nape, and sides of face light greyish brown, with a dark smudge over the eye area, and a chestnut streak from above the eye, down the sides of the face and becoming broader at the neck. Back and rump streaked with tawny and black, upper tail coverts greyish. Flight feathers are chestnut and black, tail dusky with lighter edges. The chin is black with white patches on either side, becoming streaked with black and white on lower throat, chest and flanks ash beige, belly whitish. The short thick beak is black, legs pinkish brown, eyes brown. The female lacks the chestnut streak on the side of the head, and the black on chin and throat, as can be seen in the photograph; the beak is dark above and pinkish horn below, legs and feet pinkish brown. Young birds resemble the female.

Distribution: Very common throughout the area today and essentially a bird that is always found around human habitation. Introduced at Durban and East London at the turn of the century and first recorded in Piketberg in 1962, from Vredendal in 1963, in Cape Town suburbs in 1963, and at Somerset West in 1965. Now widely distributed throughout the area but with gaps that are not understood.

Notes: A fairly tame bird found hopping around on pavements and chirping, as it perches on buildings, with a loud 'chirrip' or chissip'. When alarmed or excited the call becomes a rattling twitter. Often uses an old swallow's nest, or constructs a clumsy domed nest in a hole in a building or under an eaves, less often in a tree. Two or three broods may be reared in one season from September to March. There are between three and five eggs of very pale blue-white, heavily marked with brown, lilac and grey. In Afrikaans: Huis Mossie.

245. Cape Sparrow *Passer melanurus* 15 cm R786

Field Identification: The adult male has forehead and crown, sides of face and chin, black, with a broad white section from above the eye curving down the side of the head to the neck, and a white band around the front neck, under which is a black biblike band on the upper breast. Nape is grey with chestnut from mantle to rump. Wings are dusky edged with white, tail dusky, underparts white, with flanks tinged with grey, eyes and bill black, legs greyish. The female is grey where the male is black and the white section on the side of the head is a narrower white eyebrow stripe. The chestnut is duller. Young birds resemble the female.

Distribution: A tame and prolific resident, very numerous near human habitation and also dominant in several types of indigenous bush, favouring fairly dry country

and the drier suburbs of towns. Like the House Sparrow it is unaccountably absent from certain areas, but is found in most areas where there are trees.

Notes: Congregate in fairly large flocks when not breeding but may breed at any time of the year, usually from September to March. Sometimes do damage to spring gardens, as they feed on the soft early shoots of plants, but are nevertheless very useful as they dispose of large quantities of insects. Will also gather where grain is scattered about. This species roosts in nests all the year round so may be seen building nests at any time. The males sing a jerky song and the usual calls are 'chissip' or 'chirrip'. They build large untidy nests or sometimes use old weaver or sparrow nest, laying from three to six eggs which are white or greenish, with varying amounts of brownish markings. In Afrikaans: Mossie, in Xhosa: Undlunkulu, in Sotho: Serobele.

246. Cape Weaver *Ploceus capensis* 18 cm R799

Field Identification: The male in breeding plumage has head, neck, chest and underparts bright yellow, but with forehead, sides of face and throat washed with chestnut, hind neck streaked with olive and dusky, and chin and eye area dusky. Neck to rump is olivy green with darker centres to the feathers, tail dusky, tinged with olive green. Wings are blackish brown edged with creamy yellow. Eyes yellow, brown in female, bill black, legs pinkish grey. When not breeding the male resembles the female, having olivy beige plumage above, mottled on head, nape, and back, and with flight feathers dusky, edged with cream. There is a very slight chestnut wash, only on the sides of the head, underparts lighter. Immature birds resemble the female.

Distribution: Favours flattish country and valleys where there are trees and water. A common resident.

Notes: The forehead is often discoloured with pollen gathered when feeding on nectar from aloes and other flowers. Food is also derived from soft parts of plants, from seeds, and a variety of insects. Nests colonially but occasionally singly. The male is polygamous and builds a large hanging kidney-shaped nest for each female. He is sometimes seen fluttering his wings at the entrance calling the female to inspect the nest, but if she is not ready to lay it will be dismantled by the male, and a new one built. A large, robust species, never found in large flocks. They make a great deal of noise at the breeding site, with the male uttering a harsh 'azwit-azwit', as well as a chattering song. The alarm call is an urgent 'chit-chit-chitchit-chitchit'. Breeds from June to November with a peak in September. The female adds the lining to the nest if she accepts it, and two to five plain greenish blue eggs are laid, in which the colour is unevenly shaded over each egg, usually more intense at the thicker end. In Afrikaans: Kaapse Wewer, in Xhosa: Ihobohobo, in Sotho: Talane.

247. Masked Weaver *Ploceus velatus* 15 cm R803

Field Identification: The black mask covers forehead, sides of face, chin, and central throat of the male bird in breeding plumage. Crown to neck, sides of head and underparts are yellow with a slight chestnut wash on the crown. The mantle is a streaked olivy green, the rump yellow and the tail greyish. The wings are blackish edged with offwhite, bill black, eyes red during breeding, legs flesh coloured. The female is mottled grey green on forehead, crown and nape, sides of head greyish yellow, chin offwhite, streaked with grey, upper chest dull pale yellow, belly and underparts grey white. The mantle is olivy green, the wings dark grey, edged with offwhite, the tail grey green. Eyes are brown, bill horn, legs flesh coloured. Both sexes have red eyes when breeding. Young birds resemble the non-breeding female.

Distribution: A common species, gregarious throughout the year but usually occurring in fairly small flocks. Found chiefly in the more northern parts of the south western Cape, yet recorded several times from Rondevlei Bird Sanctuary and Zeekoe Vlei. Found breeding both at Philippi and in the Cape of Good Hope Nature Reserve. A tame species found in urban gardens and in open woodland, both in exotic and indigenous trees.

Notes: Noisy birds when gathered in a breeding colony, the male uttering a loud song described as a chattering 'swizzle'. The normal call is a 'tick-tick' and there is an alarm uttered, which is a strident 'chit-chit-chitchitchit'. The male is polygamous having two or three females during the breeding season. He builds two types of nests, one for roosting and the other for the eggs, the latter being lined by the female. Both types are suspended rounded ovals, woven from reeds or grass blades.

Eggs number two or three and vary considerably in different clutches. Some are white to pale pink, others blue white to greenish blue, plain at times, or blotched in varying amounts of grey and brown. In Afrikaans: Swartkeel-geelvink, in Xhosa: Ihobohobo, in Sotho: Talane.

248. Red Bishop *Euplectes orix* 14 cm R808

Field Identification: Male birds do not assume scarlet and black plumage seen in the photograph until the second breeding season. In full breeding plumage the forehead, forecrown, ear-coverts, breast and belly are black, flight feathers and tail black-ish dusky brown, rest of plumage bright scarlet with a slight orange wash on the back, with older males tending to become more orange. Eyes dark brown, bill black, legs pinkish. When non-breeding the male resembles the female – buff above with heavy brown streaks, light eyestripe curving down to the sides of the neck, sides of face buff lightly and finely streaked with brown, chin buff, chest and flanks buff streaked with brown, belly off-white. Eyes brown, bill and legs light brownish. Young birds re-semble the female but look a little lighter as the upper plumage has paler broad edges.

Distribution: Not often found in the immediate vicinity of Cape Town, but recorded from the Black River and Paarde Vlei. An abundant resident further north and east. Favours open country near water and become a pest in the grain growing areas when grain in ripening, as seeds and grain form a major part of their diet. Insects are caught as well, especially when feeding young birds.

Notes: Occur in small or large flocks and become very conspicuous during the breeding season from July to December, due to the spectacular colouring of the male in breeding plumage. Often nest in reeds in marshes or dongas, and also in standing corn. The male is polygamous breeding with about three females each breeding season. He constructs the shell of the oval nest with thin blades of reed, and when the eggs are first laid they can be seen through the wall of the nest. As incubation progresses the female adds soft grass seed-heads to complete the nest. Eggs usually number three and are a pale greenish blue. In Afrikaans: Rooi Kaffervink, in Xhosa: Intakomlilo, in Zulu: i-Bomvana, in Sotho: Thaka.

217

249. Yellowrumped Bishop *Euplectes capensis* 14 cm R810

Field Identification: The adult male, seen in breeding plumage, is black with a spectacular contrasting patch of bright yellow on the back and wing shoulder. Wings are black, narrowly edged with yellowish buff, forming a striped effect when the wings are folded. Eyes dark brown, bill black above pinkish white below, legs pinkish. Out of the breeding season the male resembles the female but retains the yellowish patches on upper parts and wing shoulders, as well as slightly darker wings and tail. The female is dusky brown above, including wings and tail, but with plumage on head, back and rump edged with yellowish. There is a light eyestripe, sides of face light brownish, chin buff, chest buff with centres of plumage brown, belly and underparts offwhite streaked with brown. Immature birds resemble the female. Eyes dark brown, bill blackish, legs brown.

Distribution: A resident species widely distributed but commoner on the flats than in the mountains. Found in fairly dry scrub or more usually in the marshy areas at the foot of hills or mountains.

Notes: Conspicuous with the male perched on the top of a bush in his breeding finery, keeping watch over his territory. Found in small flocks out of the breeding season, but not really colonial when nesting, as one male has a fairly large territory with three or four nesting females. The male performs a display flight accompanied by thudding wingbeats. The nest is a thick walled oval with a hooded entrance at the side near the top. The whole structure is in grass or weeds fairly near the ground. Eggs number two to four and are pale green, marked with olive and grey. The breeding season in the Cape is from August to November. In Afrikaans: Kaapse Kaffervink, in Xhosa: Isahomba.

250. Blackfaced Swee *Estrilda melanotis* 9 cm R825

Field Identification: The male is colourful and fairly glossy, with forehead, crown and nape grey, mantle and back washed with greenish yellow, upper tail coverts scarlet, tail dusky. Sides of face and chin black, contrasting with a white band

around the front throat, chest light grey, belly and underparts grey washed with light brown, flight feathers dusky. Bill is black above red below, eyes red, legs black. The female lacks the contrasting black and white on the face, being uniform grey with a slightly lighter neck, the lower bill is only slightly tinged with red and the eyes are dark brown, upper parts duller. Young birds resemble the female, but are even duller in colour.

Distribution: Extended its range into the south western Cape in 1929 and was recorded breeding at Constantia in the 1930s. Lately has been recorded only at Kirstenbosch and is rare in the Hottentots Holland, but becomes less rare further east. Inhabits the edges of forests and oak woods, but is becoming increasingly rare in the area, probably partly due to much destruction of its habitat.

Notes: Found in pairs or very small flocks either in thick bush bordering streams, or on the edges of forest land. A quiet species that is easily overlooked. Lives on soft growing grasses, grass seed and small insects. The call is a gentle 'swee-swee' or a sharp alarm call like an explosive 'tzwee'. Breeds in the area in September and the nest is made from grass stems, lined with flowering grass tops. It is a recumbent pear shape and will usually contain four pure white eggs. In Afrikaans: Swie, in Xhosa: u-Notswitswitswi.

251. Common Waxbill *Estrilda astrild* 13 cm R843

Field Identification: The outstanding characteristics for identification would be the bright red bill and eyestripe, coupled with the fine barring which extends over the entire plumage. Forehead and crown greyish, mantle, back, wings and tail grey,

finely barred with dusky, with flight feathers and tail tip rather more plain dusky. Chin and sides of neck pale grey, chest and flanks pale pinky brown barred with dusky, belly offwhite with a red streak down the centre. Eyes dark brown, legs brown. The female has less red below and young birds have even less than the female, and are barred below, with bills blackish.

Distribution: Favours open marsh country and is to be found at reedy or grassy banks of rivers and streams.

Notes: When disturbed from their feeding areas on the ground the Common Waxbill will fly off, one after the other, uttering their characteristic reedy flocking call. A lively species, continually on the move with a habit of flicking their tails from side to side, especially when disturbed. Show little fear of onlookers and may be quite tame. Feed on insects and grass seeds. The call is a 'chee-chee, churr-chit' usually taking off in flight on the 'churr'. The male utters short melodic songs. Breeding takes place during the long period from August to January, but there is a marked peak in September and October. The nest will be found in tufts of grass or even on the ground. It is round, fairly large, and has a protruding entrance measuring from seven to ten centimetres, formed from grass stems. Five or six pure white eggs are laid. The nest is not kept clean and once the young are hatched it becomes characteristically filthy. In Afrikaans: Rooibekkie, in Xhosa: in-Tshiyane, in Sotho: se-Tzetze, in Zulu: in-Tiyane.

252. Pintailed Whydah *Vidua macroura* 33 cm R846

Field Identification: The adult male in breeding plumage has forehead, eye area, crown, nape, mantle, side of breast and four elongated central tail feathers black. Throat, sides of neck, chest, belly and underparts are white, very sparsely marked with smudges of grey. Upper wing coverts are white and form a white patch on the folded black wings, clearly seen in the photograph. Rump and upper tail covers are offwhite, with side tail feathers short, and black above, with inner webs white, beautifully illustrated in this pitcture. Eyes dark brown, bill red, legs dark grey. The non-breeding male is similar to the female but is larger, rustier, and striped more heavily with black, and the bill is black.

The female has a central tawny stripe from bill to nape with two black stripes on either side, and light tawny eyebrow stripes. Sides of head, throat, and chest are beige with a blackish moustache stripe from the bill to the neck, barred with tawny. Upper plumage is dusky edged with tawny, flight feathers and tail plain dusky, flanks beige lightly streaked with brown, belly and underparts offwhite, bill reddish brown, eyes brown, legs grey. For the first two months young birds are not streaked and have black bellies, but later resemble their respective sexes in non-breeding plumage.

Distribution: Common and parasitic on the Common Waxbill, therefore found in the same localities. Favours built-up areas and farmsteads where there are plenty of trees.

Notes: A common and pugnacious species which form fairly large flocks in the non-breeding season. The male is polygamous and is seen with a number of hens, and may be in a group with a certain number of immature males still in non-breeding plumage, during the breeding season, which is from August to November. Males will sing for weeks on end, from a perch, and will drag their long tails along the ground or carry them arched gracefully in the air. An egg from the nest of the Common Waxbill, or a cisticola, will be destroyed to make room for each of the eggs of the Pintailed Whydah deposited in its place. Young birds will remain with the host's flock until old enough to fend for themselves. The eggs are pure white. In Afrikaans: Koning-rooibekkie, in Xhosa: Hlekwe, in Zulu: u-Hlegwane, in Sotho: Mmanoke.

253. Cape Siskin *Serinus tottus* 13 cm R855

Field Identification: Adult male has forehead to nape medium brown, finely streaked with black, and with a fine tawny eyebrow streak, seen clearly on the male bird in the foreground. Back, rump and upper wing coverts russet brown, flight feathers and tail black, with horizontal streaks of white on the wing tips and a ter-

minal band of white on the tail. Chin is light golden, heavily spotted with black, chest and belly dull olivy gold, under tail-coverts brown. Eyes and legs brown, bill greyish brown paler below. The female is very similar to the male but has top of head darker, as is the back, and lacks the light eyebrow stripe and gold on the throat. Young birds are similar to female, but have dusky streaks on chin and chest.

Distribution: Common in scrub on mountains and hills, and regular in Fynbos. At home in exotic pine forests.

Notes: Found in pairs or in small parties. Feed on buds, seeds and insects usually taken on a perch within a bush or shrub. In flight this species can be identified by the dark back and the white tips to the wings. The nest is often in a crevice in a rock, or in a tree trunk, as shown in the photograph, but is sometimes found in a low bush. It is made from twigs, weeds, roots and grass stems, lined with protea down or hair. Breeding takes place from September to December, when three to five greenish blue eggs are laid, speckled with reddish brown and grey at the thicker end. In Afrikaans: Pietjie-kanarie.

254. Cape Canary *Serinus canicollis* 13 cm R857

Field Identification: Adult male has forehead and crown, sides of face, centre throat, chest and belly yellow, with nape, sides of neck and sides of chest and flanks grey. The mantle is a mixture of yellow and grey, streaked with darker grey, the flight feathers dusky, washed with yellow and with lighter yellow edges, under tail co-verts and tail edges yellow, with tail shafts dusky grey. Eyes brown, bill greyish-brown above and greyish-yellow below, legs grey. The female, seen on the nest, is similar but duller and more streaked, as are immature birds.

Distribution: Frequents areas adjacent to the scrub and forest of the mountains. Its habitat overlaps to some extent with the Yellow Canary, but this species is also found on the mountains, where the Yellow Canary is rare or absent.

Notes: Common and found most often in large flocks, especially towards evening

when they gather to roost. The flight pattern is undulating with frequent wingbeats. Flocks break up during the breeding season, from July to December, and especially in September, to form mating pairs. During this time the male has a flapping display flight and will sing in flight. Cape Canaries are seedeaters, living on the soft green seeds of shrubs and weeds. The usual call is a full ascending 'tsweet' and this species is considered the best songster of the Canary family, with a loud melodic song similar to that of the English Lark. The nest is shaped like a small basin, made from tendrils and pliable grass stalks, warmly lined with cosy vegetation. It is usually about six metres from the ground in a tall bush or tree and is built entirely by the female. Eggs number three or four, white with a greenish tinge, marked at the thicker end with reddish brown and grey. In Afrikaans: Kaapse Kanarie, in Zulu: um-Zwilili, in Xhosa: u-Longi, in Sotho:Tsoere.

255. Blackheaded Canary *Serinus alario* 14 cm R861

Field Identification: This outstanding photograph shows the male feeding the female on the nest. The adult male has the entire head, chin, and throat to upper breast plain black. The amount of black on the breast varies from bird to bird. There is an offwhite band around the hind neck and down the sides of the neck to the underparts, which are slightly streaked with grey and chestnut. Back, rump, tail, and upper wing-coverts are chestnut with primaries blackish. Eyes dark brown, bill grey, lighter below, legs dark grey. The female is greyish on head and neck with dusky streaks, wing shoulder and upper parts chestnut, underparts buff to offwhite. Young birds resemble the female but are more streaked.

Distribution: Fairly common in the drier karoo-type areas but rare in the Peninsula.

Notes: Found feeding on seeds, taken mainly from the ground, either singly, in pairs, or in small parties. The call is quieter than most other seedeaters, being a gentle 'tweet' or 'sweea'. Considered chiefly a visitor, present from July to October, nesting from August to October. A small cup-shaped nest is built in a bush or small tree, about a metre from the ground. It is lined with vegetable down and will contain three to five eggs of greenish-white, with scattered marks of varying shades of brown. In Afrikaans: Swartkop-kanarie.

256. Bully Canary *Serinus sulphuratus* 15 cm R863

Field Identification: Adult male, seen in the photograph, has forehead, crown, nape, mantle, back, and rump, dull olivy green with dusky streaks on all but the rump; flight and tail feathers blackish, edged with light olivy beige. sides of face and

neck are also dull olivy green, with bright canary yellow on eyebrow stripe, on side of neck, and at chin and throat. Underparts dull olivy yellow. The stout arched bill is greyish horn, eyes dark brown, legs grey. The female is somewhat duller and more heavily streaked. Young birds resemble the female but are streaked on sides of breast and flanks as well.

Distribution: Found in open coastal bush, and grassland with trees, but more numerous in the mountains, including suburban gardens cultivated on the slopes of mountains.

Notes: Seen singly or in pairs feeding on the ground, hopping about very briskly with an upright stance. The Bully Canary has a fairly heavy build and a rapid and less undulating flight than other canary species. Forms small flocks during the winter months, which break up into mating pairs for the July to November breeding season. Food is derived from seeds and buds. The call is less musical than that expected from a canary, and is a deep 'sqeerk' or a rasping 'chirr-irr-ree', also a rather deep unmusical song. the nest is a shallow basin lined with softer material, containing two to four greenish white eggs, sometimes having a few brown marks at the thicker end. In Afrikaans: Geel Dikbek-sysie, in Xhosa: i-Ndweza eluhlaza.

257. Whitethroated Seedeater *Serinus albogularis* 15 cm R865

Field Identification: Has a very heavy lower bill, this coupled with the pale ashy brown of the head and mantle, the white eyebrow stripe, white sparsely streaked throat and yellow rump make identification unmistakable. Upper parts are lightly streaked, tail and flight feathers dusky with narrow offwhite edges, underparts pale greyish white. Eyes brown, bill horn, legs mottled brown and flesh. Females and young birds are similar.

Distribution: Widely distributed and common resident in dry areas, favouring scrub country on hillsides and dry river beds, but not forest lands. Fairly frequent in cultivation.

Notes: Usually found in pairs or small parties. When not breeding small flocks may be in the company of Bully Canaries. Flight pattern is swift and direct, and when hopping around on the ground feeding, it is seen to be a thick-set bird in contrast to the slender Streakyheaded Seedeater. The nest, as seen in the illustration, is the typical shallow bowl of the canaries, made from twigs and rootlets and lined with vegetable down. Two to four eggs are laid usually an immaculate greenish white, but occasionally marked at the thicker end with purplish black. In Afrikaans: Witkeel-dikbek-sysie.

258. Yellow Canary *Serinus flaviventris* R866

Field Identification: Centre crown and nape, hind part of sides of face, mantle, back and rump dull olivy yellow; eyebrow stripe, forepart of sides of face, throat, belly and underparts, as well as upper tail-coverts canary yellow, the latter being washed with grey. Flight and tail feathers greyish black edged with yellow. Eyes dark brown, bill greyish horn, legs grey. The female is more streaked and young birds resemble the female but are duller in colour.

Distribution: A common resident species found in indigenous bush and in cultivated areas, especially in the flatter terrain. Favour open woodland near water. Found in coastal scrub, and even right on the beach, or perched on rocks in the sea.

Notes: During the winter months they are seen in small flocks, but either singly or in pairs from July to November, the breeding season in the south western Cape. Seeds and termites form their food. The call is a high-pitched 'tirriyip', the males being good singers. A typical Yellow Canary nest is built in a low bush or tree, and three or four greenish white eggs are laid, usually, but not always, boldly spotted or streaked at the thick end, with dark brown or black. In Afrikaans: Geelsysie.

259. Streakyheaded Seedeater *Serinus gularis* 15 cm R867

Field Identification: Head, neck and sides of face ashy brown, streaked with blackish and white. Back, with dusky streaks, rump, wings and tail, ashy brown, with flight feathers and the tips of tail feathers darker. There is a very prominent white eyebrow stripe. Underparts lighter ashy brown. Eyes dark brown, longish thick bill grey above and pinkish horn below, legs greyish brown. Females are similar, young birds streaked on mantle.

Distribution: Frequents open woodland and tall scrub, and is found in urban gardens. Fairly common in Swellendam and Bredasdorp.

Notes: An unobtrusive bird seen perched on seedheads, pecking at the seeds, particularly of opening pine cones. Apart from seeds, flower buds, petals, termites and caterpillars form part of the diet. Sings in a quiet way, either a husky 'chirrit' or a 'see-e-ee'. September to April is the breeding season, when a cup-shaped nest is formed from grass and leaf stems, bound together with cobwebs and lined with soft vegetable down. Two to four greenish white eggs, speckled sparsely with pink and brown at the thicker end, are laid. In Afrikaans: Streepkop-sysie, in Xhosa: i-Ndweze.

260. Protea Seedeater *Serinus leucopterus* 15 cm R869

Field Identification: Similar to the Whitethroated Seedeater but can be distinguished in the field by the plain light brown rump. Has a faint white eyebrow and two white bars on the dusky wings formed by a white edge to the feathers, visible at rest but not in flight, and clearly seen in the photograph. Upper parts are light brown streaked with dusky, wings and tail dusky. Eye area, forehead and chin, are darker brown, throat white, chest, belly and underparts light ash brown. The arched bill is pinkish horn, almost white at the base, eyes dark brown, legs pinkish brown.

Distribution: Described as rare but actually fairly common in suitable areas. A mountain species associated with Protea bush country, resident where it occurs, but not resident on the Cape Peninsula in general. Confined to the mountains of the south west Cape from Niewoudtville southwards to Cape Hangklip, and eastwards to the Baviaanskloof.

Notes: Usually hidden in thick vegetation and will be found in heavily vegetated kloofs in the mountains. When disturbed will fly low over the bushes and take cover as quickly as possible. Occur in pairs or singly. Live on dried ericas, the seeds of pro-teas and various other plants. The call is a soft, melodic, 'tree-loo-loo' or a 'sweet' like the Cape Canary. Breeds from August to October, the cup-shaped nest being made of dried stems, grass and protea down, usually well hidden in the fork of a Protea bush or Pine tree – although the nest in the picture looks fairly well exposed. Eggs number two to four, either ivory or pale blue, glossy, and with black, purple and brown marks at the thicker end. In Afrikaans: Witvlerk-sysie.

261. Larklike Bunting *Emberiza impetuani* 14 cm R871

Field Identification: Head greyish buff with dusky streaks on central forehead, crown and nape, and a light eyebrow stripe. Chin and throat greyish white, upper bill grey, larger lower bill horn, back tawny buff with heavy dusky streaks, flight and tail feathers dusky with lighter tawny beige edges, underparts buff with belly lighter. Females and young birds are similar. The small head is not patterned in black and white like other buntings, and there is no white on the wing or tail feathers.

Distribution: Common in the dry northern parts of this area favouring open country. Not present in Cape Town though occurring as far south west as Vissershoek. Particularly common in the Karoo.

Notes: Thought to be a breeding summer migrant nesting in September and October. The nest is built by the female, using grass and roots, and may be found in the open or in a patch of weeds and grass. Two to four eggs are laid, coloured greenish white and spotted with brown. This species lives on seeds and insects, and the call is a plaintive nasal-toned 'chut'. Males utter a courtship song from the tops of bushes, which is rather guttural and monotonous, ending on a wheezy tone. Spends most of its time on the ground and may be seen in great numbers at water holes in the cool of the evening. In Afrikaans: Vaal Streepkoppie.

262. Cape Bunting *Emberiza capensis* 13 cm R873

Field Identification: Central forehead, crown and nape, as well as mantle and back, light greyish brown, streaked with black. Sides of face offwhite, with thick black eye and moustache stripes. Chin and throat whitish, underparts light grey, wings dusky with shoulder and broad edges chestnut, tail feathers dusky, edged with chestnut. Eyes brown, bill and legs grey. Females are similar and young birds somewhat duller with dusky streaks on chest.

Distribution: Resident in all types of indigenous bush both in mountainous country and in rocky, sandy coastal regions.

Notes: A fairly tame, common species often found near human habitation; seen in pairs or parties, less often singly. Flies for short distances fairly near the ground and when walking or hopping along the ground, looking for seeds, grasshoppers, beetles or spiders, has a squat plump appearance, and a shuffling movement. Will perch on a rock singing its shrill canary type song while opening and closing its wings in characteristic fashion. Other calls are a chirp similar to that of a sparrow and a loud 'cherowee'. Breeding takes place from August to November in the south western Cape, and a bowl shaped nest, made from fine roots and grass, is built in a small bush or tuft of grass. Eggs, usually numbering three, but occasionally two or four, are white with markings of pinky brown and purplish grey extending over the entire surface. In Afrikaans: Streepkoppie, in Sotho: Mborokoane.

BIBLIOGRAPHY

CAPE BIRD CLUB. 1981. *A Guide to the Birds of the S.W. Cape.*

FINCH-DAVIES C.G. & KEMP A.C. 1981. *The Birds of Prey of Southern Africa.*

LOCKWOOD G. 1981. *Geoff Lockwood's Garden Birds of Southern Africa.*

McLACHLAN & LIVERSIDGE. 1978. *Robert's Birds of South Africa.*

NEWMAN K. 1979. *Birdlife in Southern Africa.*

PROUT-JONES D.V. 1974. *An Introduction to the Birds of Prey of South Africa.*

PROZESKY O.P.M. 1980. *A Field Guide to the Birds of Southern Africa.*

READER'S DIGEST SERVICES (PTY) LTD. 1976. *Reader's Digest Complete Book of Australian Birds.*

SKEAD C.J. 1967. *Sunbirds of Southern Africa.*

SOUTH AFRICAN ORNITHOLOGICAL SOCIETY. 1980. *SAOS Checklist of Southern African Birds.*

WINTERBOTTOM J.M. 1971. *Priests Eggs of Southern African Birds (Revised)*

INDEX — *English Bird Names*

INDEX — *Afrikaans Bird Names*

xvii

The Afrikaans names reflected in this index represent traditional usage over many years, and the authoress has decided to retain this nomenclature.